SIMPLE & DELICIOUS®

TASTE OF HOME BOOKS • RDA ENTHUSIAST BRANDS, LLC • MILWAUKEE, WI

CILANTRO LIME SHRIMP, 67

Cover Photographer: Jim Wieland
Cover Food Stylist: Lauren Knoelke
Cover Set Stylist: Melissa Franco

Pictured on front cover: Pizza in a Bowl, page 59
Pictured on back cover: Spaghetti Squash Meatball Casserole, page 107; Black Bean Turkey Chili, page 40; Spring Asparagus, page 152
Pictured on title page: Blue Cheese Potato Chips, page 27
Pictured on spine: Raspberry Chocolate Puffs, page 226

1610 N. 2nd St., Suite 102, Milwaukee WI 53212-3906

International Standard Book Number: 978-1-61765-751-1
Library of Congress Control Number: 2017963392

Printed in USA
1 3 5 7 9 10 8 6 4 2

APPLE DUMPLING BAKE, 223

CONTENTS

5, 10, 15-Minute Favorites 6

30-Minute Wonders 38

5-Ingredient Entrees 68

Meal-in-One Mainstays 98

Sides, Salads & More 130

Soups & Sandwiches 162

Slow-Cooked Greats 192

Easily Impressive Desserts 224

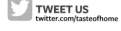

Index 254

CASHEW TURKEY SALAD SANDWICHES, 180

THAI COCONUT BEEF, 198

BUCATINI WITH SAUSAGE & KALE, 74

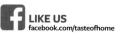

ITALIAN JOES ON TEXAS TOAST, 63

Memorable Dishes Are Just Moments Away

Today's cooks know how to get dinner on the table even on their busiest nights. Now they're sharing those secrets with you in this must-have cookbook, Taste of Home Simple & Delicious!

Inside, you'll find 115 of the recipes family cooks rely on **when time is tight.** Turn the page and see for yourself! You'll discover dishes that are table-ready in as little as 10 minutes, comforting meal-in-one entrees, fantastic five-ingredient main courses and slow cooker classics that make dinner available when you are.

Need to round out meals quickly? Don't worry! There are dozens of no-fuss side dishes, salads and soups that complement menus. Looking for a dessert that won't eat up too much kitchen time? You're covered with an entire chapter of treats that beat the clock and steal the spotlight.

SLOW COOKER SRIRACHA CORN, 194

EASY BERRY CHEESECAKE PARFAITS, 229

Throughout the book, you'll see two **At-a-Glance Icons** that make it even easier to find recipes that fit your schedule.

5 INGREDIENTS These dishes come together with five or fewer ingredients, not including water, salt, pepper, oils or optional items.

FREEZE IT A little planning leads to a freezer full of fast meals when you look for these make-ahead greats.

JALAPENO BURGERS WITH GORGONZOLA, 171

Best of all, every recipe includes a full-color photo, offers a complete set of nutrition facts and features large-print type. You'll never struggle to read measurements again! With this **Simple & Delicious** cookbook, you're only minutes away from enjoying a new family favorite.

Blue Cheese
Potato Chips, p. 27

CHAPTER 1

5, 10, 15-MINUTE FAVORITES

Short on time? You can still make a great bite that's long on flavor.

Cannellini Bean Hummus 8
Snappy Tuna Melts 11
Pina Colada Dip 12
Spinach Blueberry Salad. 15
Roasted Red Pepper Tapenade 16
Catherine's Guacamole 20
Cucumbers with Dressing. 23
Cobb Salad Sub 24
Blue Cheese Potato Chips. 27
Strawberry Watermelon Slush. 28
Sun-Dried Tomato Garlic Bread 31
Berries in Yogurt Cream 32
Broccoli Slaw 35
Caprese Salad Kabobs. 36

Cannellini Bean Hummus

My white-bean hummus features a delightful nuttiness from tahini, a peanut butter-like paste made from ground sesame seeds that's a staple ingredient in traditional hummus. The beans pack a lot of protein, so it's a healthy snack for kids.
—MARINA CASTLE KELLEY CANYON COUNTRY, CA

START TO FINISH: 5 MIN.
MAKES: 1¼ CUPS

- **2 garlic cloves, peeled**
- **1 can (15 ounces) white kidney or cannellini beans, rinsed and drained**
- **¼ cup tahini**
- **3 tablespoons lemon juice**
- **1½ teaspoons ground cumin**
- **¼ teaspoon salt**
- **¼ teaspoon crushed red pepper flakes**
- **2 tablespoons minced fresh parsley**
- **Pita breads, cut into wedges**
- **Assorted fresh vegetables**

1. Place garlic in a food processor; cover and process until minced. Add the beans, tahini, lemon juice, cumin, salt and pepper flakes; cover and process until smooth.

2. Transfer to a small bowl; stir in parsley. Refrigerate until serving. Serve with pita wedges and assorted fresh vegetables.

NUTRITION FACTS 2 tablespoons (calculated without pita bread or vegetables): 78 cal., 4g fat (1g sat. fat), 0 chol., 114mg sod., 8g carb. (0 sugars, 2g fiber), 3g pro. ***Diabetic Exchanges:*** 1 fat, ½ starch.

Snappy Tuna Melts

I lightened up a tuna melt by switching mayo to creamy balsamic vinaigrette. Kids and adults both go for this delicious, quick meal.

—**CHRISTINE SCHENHER** EXETER, CA

START TO FINISH: 15 MIN.
MAKES: 4 SERVINGS

- **1 pouch (11 ounces) light tuna in water**
- **1 hard-boiled large egg, coarsely chopped**
- **2 tablespoons reduced-fat creamy balsamic vinaigrette**
- **1 tablespoon stone-ground mustard, optional**
- **4 whole wheat hamburger buns, split**
- **8 slices tomato**
- **8 slices reduced-fat Swiss cheese**

1. In a small bowl, mix tuna, egg, vinaigrette and, if desired, mustard. Place buns on an ungreased baking sheet, cut side up. Broil 4-6 in. from heat 1-2 minutes or until golden brown.

2. Spread the tuna mixture over buns; top with tomato and cheese. Broil 2-3 minutes longer or until the cheese is melted.

NUTRITION FACTS 2 open-faced sandwiches (calculated without mustard): 341 cal., 13g fat (5g sat. fat), 105mg chol., 557mg sod., 27g carb. (6g sugars, 4g fiber), 35g pro. ***Diabetic Exchanges:*** 4 lean meat, 2 starch, 1 fat.

Pina Colada Dip

If you like pina coladas, you've gotta try this fluffy fruit dip. Scooped up with a slice of fresh pineapple, it tastes just like the beloved beachside drink.

—*TASTE OF HOME* TEST KITCHEN

PREP: 10 MIN. + CHILLING
MAKES: 20 SERVINGS

1¼ cups cold 2% milk
¾ cup (6 ounces) pineapple yogurt
1 package (3.4 ounces) instant coconut cream pudding mix
1 carton (8 ounces) frozen whipped topping, thawed
Toasted unsweetened coconut flakes and maraschino cherries, optional
Fresh pineapple wedges
Vanilla wafers

1. In a large bowl, whisk milk, yogurt and pudding mix for 2 minutes (mixture will be thick). Fold in whipped topping. Refrigerate, covered, at least 2 hours.

2. If desired, top with coconut and cherries before serving. Serve with pineapple wedges and wafers.

NUTRITION FACTS ¼ cup dip: 68 cal., 3g fat (3g sat. fat), 2mg chol., 64mg sod., 8g carb. (8g sugars, 0 fiber), 1g pro.

Spinach Blueberry Salad

Blueberries are a fun surprise in this salad. I received the recipe from a co-worker's wife, and it's become one of my favorites.

—**HEIDI GILLELAND** LEE'S SUMMIT, MO

START TO FINISH: 15 MIN.
MAKES: 8 SERVINGS

1/4 cup raspberry vinegar
2 teaspoons Dijon mustard
1 teaspoon sugar
1/2 teaspoon salt
1/2 cup canola oil

SALAD

12 cups fresh baby spinach (about 10 ounces)
1 cup fresh blueberries
1 cup crumbled blue cheese
1/2 cup chopped pecans, toasted

Mix the first four ingredients; gradually whisk in the oil until blended. In a large bowl, combine salad ingredients; toss with dressing.

NOTE To toast nuts, bake in a shallow pan in a 350° oven for 5-10 minutes or cook in a skillet over low heat until lightly browned, stirring occasionally.

NUTRITION FACTS 1 serving: 254 cal., 24g fat (5g sat. fat), 13mg chol., 407mg sod., 6g carb. (3g sugars, 2g fiber), 6g pro.

Roasted Red Pepper Tapenade

When entertaining, I often rely on my pepper tapenade recipe because it takes only 15 minutes to whip up and pop in the fridge. Sometimes I swap out the almonds for walnuts or pecans.

—**DONNA MAGLIARO** DENVILLE, NJ

PREP: 15 MIN. + CHILLING
MAKES: 2 CUPS

- 3 garlic cloves, peeled
- 2 cups roasted sweet red peppers, drained
- ½ cup blanched almonds
- ⅓ cup tomato paste
- 2 tablespoons olive oil
- ¼ teaspoon salt
- ¼ teaspoon pepper
- Minced fresh basil
- Toasted French bread baguette slices or water crackers

1. In a small saucepan, bring 2 cups water to a boil. Add garlic; cook, uncovered, 6-8 minutes or just until tender. Drain and pat dry. Place red peppers, almonds, tomato paste, oil, garlic, salt and pepper in a small food processor; process until blended. Transfer to a small bowl. Refrigerate at least 4 hours to allow flavors to blend.

2. Sprinkle with basil. Serve with baguette slices.

NUTRITION FACTS 2 tablespoons dip: 58 cal., 4g fat (0 sat. fat), 0 chol., 152mg sod., 3g carb. (2g sugars, 1g fiber), 1g pro. ***Diabetic Exchanges:*** 1 fat.

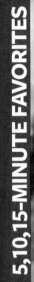

Nuts & Seeds Trail Mix

There is plenty of protein and fiber in a handful of this combo, making it a great instant energy boost while also being a bit of an indulgence.

—KRISTIN RIMKUS SNOHOMISH, WA

START TO FINISH: 5 MIN.
MAKES: 5 CUPS

- **1 cup salted pumpkin seeds or pepitas**
- **1 cup unblanched almonds**
- **1 cup unsalted sunflower kernels**
- **1 cup walnut halves**
- **1 cup dried apricots**
- **1 cup dark chocolate chips**

Place all ingredients in a large bowl; toss to combine. Store in an airtight container.

NUTRITION FACTS ⅓ cup: 336 cal., 25g fat (6g sat. fat), 0 chol., 96mg sod., 22g carb. (13g sugars, 4g fiber), 11g pro.

TOP TIP

To keep this mix, follow the general guidelines for storing nuts: Store in an airtight container in a cool place. Shelled nuts can be refrigerated for up to 4 months and frozen for up to 8 months.

Catherine's Guacamole

Get the scoop on making a standout guacamole. A handful of chopped celery adds some fun crunch in this avocado dip—everyone's favorite fiesta starter.
—**CATHERINE CASSIDY** MILWAUKEE, WI

PREP: 15 MIN. + CHILLING
MAKES: 2½ CUPS

3 medium ripe avocados, peeled and pitted
⅓ cup chopped sweet onion
1 small tomato, seeded and chopped
1 celery rib, finely chopped
2 garlic cloves, minced
2 tablespoons lemon or lime juice
2 teaspoons Worcestershire sauce
½ teaspoon salt
¼ teaspoon pepper
¼ to ⅓ cup chopped fresh cilantro, optional
Tortilla chips

In a small bowl, mash avocados. Stir in onion, tomato, celery, garlic, lemon juice, Worcestershire, salt, pepper and, if desired, cilantro. Chill 1 hour before serving. Serve with chips.

NUTRITION FACTS ¼ cup (calculated without chips): 75 cal., 6g fat (1g sat. fat), 0 chol., 136mg sod., 5g carb. (1g sugars, 3g fiber), 1g pro. ***Diabetic Exchanges:*** 1 fat.

(5) INGREDIENTS

Cucumbers with Dressing

It wouldn't be summer if Mom didn't make lots of these creamy cucumbers. Just a few simple ingredients—mayonnaise, sugar, vinegar and salt—dress up slices of this crisp garden vegetable.

—MICHELLE BERAN CLAFLIN, KS

PREP: 10 MIN. + CHILLING
MAKES: 6 SERVINGS

- **1 cup mayonnaise**
- **¼ cup sugar**
- **¼ cup white vinegar**
- **¼ teaspoon salt**
- **4 cups thinly sliced cucumbers**

In a large bowl, mix first four ingredients; toss with cucumbers. Refrigerate, covered, 2 hours.

NUTRITION FACTS ¾ cup: 283 cal., 27g fat (4g sat. fat), 3mg chol., 286mg sod., 11g carb. (10g sugars, 0 fiber), 0 pro.

TOP TIP

If you want the cucumbers in your salad to be cool and crunchy, just chill them overnight in ice water. You'll be delighted with the results...and so will everyone else!
—Ruby W., Bogalusa, LA

Cobb Salad Sub

When we need a quick meal to share, we turn Cobb salad into a sandwich masterpiece. Sometimes I swap out the bread for tortillas and make wraps instead.

—KIMBERLY GRUSENDORF MEDINA, OH

START TO FINISH: 15 MIN.
MAKES: 12 SERVINGS

- **1 loaf (1 pound) unsliced Italian bread**
- **½ cup balsamic vinaigrette or dressing of your choice**
- **5 ounces fresh baby spinach (about 6 cups)**
- **1½ pounds sliced deli ham**
- **4 hard-boiled large eggs, finely chopped**
- **8 bacon strips, cooked and crumbled**
- **½ cup crumbled Gorgonzola cheese**
- **1 cup cherry tomatoes, chopped**

Cut loaf of bread in half horizontally; hollow out both top and bottom, leaving a ¾-in. shell (discard the removed bread or save it for another use). Brush vinaigrette over bread halves. Layer spinach, ham, eggs, bacon, cheese and tomatoes on the bottom half of the bread. Replace the top. Cut in half lengthwise; cut crosswise five times to make 12 total pieces.

NUTRITION FACTS 1 piece: 233 cal., 10g fat (3g sat. fat), 97mg chol., 982mg sod., 17g carb. (3g sugars, 1g fiber), 18g pro.

5 INGREDIENTS

Blue Cheese Potato Chips

Game day calls for something bold. I top crunchy potato chips with tomatoes, bacon and tangy blue cheese. I make two big pans, and they always disappear.

—**BONNIE HAWKINS** ELKHORN, WI

START TO FINISH: 15 MIN.
MAKES: 10 SERVINGS

- **1 package (8½ ounces) kettle-cooked potato chips**
- **2 medium tomatoes, seeded and chopped**
- **8 bacon strips, cooked and crumbled**
- **6 green onions, chopped**
- **1 cup crumbled blue cheese**

1. Preheat broiler. In a 15x10x1-in. baking pan, arrange potato chips in an even layer. Top with the remaining ingredients.

2. Broil 4-5 in. from heat 2-3 minutes or until cheese begins to melt. Serve immediately.

NUTRITION FACTS 1 serving: 215 cal., 14g fat (5g sat. fat), 17mg chol., 359mg sod., 16g carb. (2g sugars, 1g fiber), 6g pro.

(5) INGREDIENTS

Strawberry Watermelon Slush

When the summer days are at their longest and hottest, we like to relax on the back porch with glasses of my slush. Strawberries and watermelon blend with lemon juice and sugar for an icy treat that's an instant refresher.
—**PATTY HOWSE** GREAT FALLS, MT

START TO FINISH: 10 MIN.
MAKES: 4 SERVINGS

- **1⁄3 cup lemon juice**
- **1⁄3 cup sugar**
- **2 cups cubed seedless watermelon**
- **2 cups fresh strawberries, halved**
- **2 cups ice cubes**

Place the first four ingredients in a blender; cover and process until smooth. Add ice; process, covered, until slushy. Serve immediately.

NUTRITION FACTS 1¼ cups: 112 cal., 0 fat (0 sat. fat), 0 chol., 4mg sod., 30g carb. (27g sugars, 2g fiber), 1g pro.

5 INGREDIENTS

Sun-Dried Tomato Garlic Bread

My fast bread recipe tastes terrific with a variety of main courses. It comes together in minutes—easy enough for a weekday but special enough for weekend guests.

—NADINE MESCH MOUNT HEALTHY, OH

START TO FINISH: 10 MIN.
MAKES: 6 SERVINGS

- **¼ cup butter, softened**
- **¼ cup grated Parmesan cheese**
- **2 tablespoons chopped oil-packed sun-dried tomatoes**
- **1 to 2 garlic cloves, minced**
- **½ loaf Italian bread, halved lengthwise**

1. In a small bowl, combine the butter, cheese, tomatoes and garlic. Spread over cut sides of bread. Transfer to an ungreased baking sheet.

2. Broil 4 in. from the heat for 3-4 minutes or until golden brown. Cut into slices and serve warm.

NUTRITION FACTS 1 slice: 189 cal., 10g fat (6g sat. fat), 23mg chol., 332mg sod., 20g carb. (0 sugars, 1g fiber), 5g pro.

5 INGREDIENTS

Berries in Yogurt Cream

Yogurt, cream, brown sugar and fresh fruit are all you need to wake up your taste buds on mornings you'd rather sleep in. Save time by having guests assemble their own parfaits.
—MICHELLE STILLMAN LANCASTER, PA

PREP: 10 MIN. + CHILLING
MAKES: 10 SERVINGS

1½ cups (12 ounces) plain yogurt
1¼ cups heavy whipping cream
½ cup packed brown sugar
5 cups assorted fresh berries

1. Place yogurt in a large bowl; whisk in cream. Sprinkle with brown sugar but do not stir. Cover and refrigerate for at least 3 hours.

2. Just before serving, stir cream mixture. Divide among 10 dessert dishes. Top with berries.

NUTRITION FACTS ¾ cup (½ cup berries with ¼ cup cream mixture): 208 cal., 12g fat (8g sat. fat), 46mg chol., 33mg sod., 24g carb. (20g sugars, 2g fiber), 2g pro.

Broccoli Slaw

Here's a sweet, new twist on traditional coleslaw. It's so easy to make and has an irresistible tangy crunch.
—**KONNY THOMAS** CITRUS HEIGHTS, CA

PREP: 15 MIN. + CHILLING
MAKES: 6 SERVINGS

4 cups broccoli florets
2 cups shredded red cabbage
1 small sweet onion, finely chopped
1 medium carrot, shredded
1/2 cup raisins
1 cup coleslaw salad dressing

In a large bowl, combine all the ingredients and toss. Refrigerate, covered, at least 2 hours. Stir before serving.

NUTRITION FACTS 1 cup: 225 cal., 12g fat (2g sat. fat), 4mg chol., 325mg sod., 25g carb. (19g sugars, 3g fiber), 3g pro.

DID YOU KNOW?

When storing sweet onions, keep them cool, dry and separate. Place them in a single layer, wrapped separately in foil or paper towels, in the vegetable bin of the refrigerator. Otherwise, store them in the coolest area of your home with good air circulation.

(5) INGREDIENTS

Caprese Salad Kabobs

Trade in the usual veggie party platter for these fun kabobs. I often make these for my family to snack on; it's a great recipe for the kids to help with.

—**CHRISTINE MITCHELL** GLENDORA, CA

START TO FINISH: 10 MIN.
MAKES: 12 KABOBS

- **24 grape tomatoes**
- **12 cherry-size fresh mozzarella cheese balls**
- **24 fresh basil leaves**
- **2 tablespoons olive oil**
- **2 teaspoons balsamic vinegar**

On each of 12 appetizer skewers, alternately thread two tomatoes, one cheese ball and two basil leaves. To serve, whisk together oil and vinegar; drizzle over kabobs.

NUTRITION FACTS 1 kabob: 44 cal., 4g fat (1g sat. fat), 5mg chol., 10mg sod., 2g carb. (1g sugars, 0 fiber), 1g pro. ***Diabetic Exchanges:*** 1 fat.

Southwest-Style Wedding Soup, p. 51

CHAPTER 2

30-MINUTE WONDERS

In just half an hour, you can have a delicious, home-cooked meal on your table!

Black Bean Turkey Chili. 40

Glazed Smoked Chops with Pears 43

Jalapeno Popper Mexican Street Corn . . . 44

Grilled Chicken, Mango &
Blue Cheese Tortillas. 47

White Cheddar Mac & Cheese 48

Southwest-Style Wedding Soup 51

Grilled Eggplant Sandwiches 52

Vegetarian Pad Thai 55

Maple-Dijon Chicken. 56

Pizza in a Bowl 59

Greek Couscous Salad. 60

Italian Joes on Texas Toast. 63

Grilled Garden Pizza 64

Cilantro Lime Shrimp 67

FREEZE IT

Black Bean Turkey Chili

This busy-day chili is packed with flavor. We make it ahead and put some in the freezer for future meals.

—**MARISELA SEGOVIA** MIAMI, FL

START TO FINISH: 30 MIN.
MAKES: 6 SERVINGS

- 1 pound lean ground turkey
- 1 large green pepper, chopped
- 1 medium onion, chopped
- 2 tablespoons chili powder
- ½ teaspoon salt
- ¼ teaspoon pepper
- ⅛ to ¼ teaspoon cayenne pepper
- 1 can (15 ounces) no-salt-added tomato sauce
- 1 can (15 ounces) black beans, rinsed and drained
- 1½ cups frozen corn (about 8 ounces), thawed
- 1 large tomato, chopped
- ½ cup water
- Shredded cheddar cheese, optional

1. In a 6-qt stockpot, cook and crumble turkey with green pepper and onion over medium-high heat until turkey is no longer pink, 5-7 minutes.

2. Stir in seasonings; cook 1 minute. Stir in tomato sauce, beans, corn, tomato and water; bring to a boil. Reduce heat; simmer, uncovered, to allow the flavors to blend, about 10 minutes, stirring occasionally. If desired, serve with shredded cheese.

FREEZE OPTION Freeze cooled chili in freezer containers. To use, partially thaw in refrigerator overnight. Heat through in a saucepan, stirring occasionally and adding a little water if necessary.

NUTRITION FACTS 1 cup: 247 cal., 7g fat (2g sat. fat), 52mg chol., 468mg sod., 27g carb. (7g sugars, 7g fiber), 21g pro. ***Diabetic Exchanges:*** 3 lean meat, 1½ starch, 1 vegetable.

Glazed Smoked Chops with Pears

My husband would eat pork chops every day if he could. Luckily, they're good all sorts of ways, so they're never boring. This recipe matches sweet pears with smoky chops.
—LYNN MORETTI OCONOMOWOC, WI

START TO FINISH: 30 MIN.
MAKES: 4 SERVINGS

- **4 smoked boneless pork chops**
- **1 tablespoon olive oil**
- **1 large sweet onion, cut into thin wedges**
- **½ cup dry red wine or reduced-sodium chicken broth**
- **2 tablespoons balsamic vinegar**
- **2 tablespoons honey**
- **2 large ripe pears, cut into 1-inch wedges**

1. Preheat oven to 350°. In an ovenproof skillet over medium-high heat, brown the pork chops on both sides; remove from pan.

2. In same pan, heat oil over medium heat; saute onion until tender, 3-5 minutes. Add wine, vinegar and honey; bring to a boil, stirring to loosen any browned bits from the pan. Reduce heat; simmer, uncovered, until slightly thickened, about 5 minutes, stirring occasionally.

3. Return chops to pan; top with pears. Transfer to oven; bake until pears are tender, 10-15 minutes.

NUTRITION FACTS 1 serving: 313 cal., 4g fat (6g sat. fat), 41mg chol., 1056mg sod., 34g carb. (26g sugars, 4g fiber), 22g pro.

TOP TIP

When choosing pears for cooking, avoid fruit with bruises, soft spots or cuts; pick ones that feel firm to the touch. These fruits will hold up better against an oven's heat. Bosc, Anjou and Bartlett pears are ideal for cooking.

Jalapeno Popper Mexican Street Corn

One of the best things about summer is fresh sweet corn. This recipe is a definite standout—we love its creamy dressing, crunchy panko coating and spicy jalapeno kick. If you're really feeling wild, sprinkle these delicious ears with a bit of cooked and crumbled bacon!

—CRYSTAL SCHLUETER BABBITT, MN

START TO FINISH: 30 MIN.
MAKES: 4 SERVINGS

- **4 ears fresh sweet corn**
- **2 jalapeno peppers**
- **3 tablespoons canola oil, divided**
- **¾ teaspoon salt, divided**
- **¼ cup panko (Japanese) bread crumbs**
- **½ teaspoon smoked paprika**
- **½ teaspoon dried Mexican oregano**
- **4 ounces cream cheese, softened**
- **¼ cup media crema table cream or sour cream thinned with 1 teaspoon 2% milk**
- **2 tablespoons lime juice**
- **Ground chipotle pepper or chili powder**
- **Chopped fresh cilantro, optional**

1. Husk corn. Rub corn and jalapenos with 2 tablespoons canola oil. Grill, covered, on a greased grill rack over medium-high direct heat until lightly charred on all sides, 10-12 minutes. Remove from heat. When the jalapenos are cool enough to handle, remove skin, seeds and membranes; chop finely. Set aside.

2. Sprinkle corn with ½ teaspoon salt. In a small skillet, heat remaining oil over medium heat. Add panko; cook and stir until starting to brown. Add paprika and oregano; cook until crumbs are toasted and fragrant.

3. Meanwhile, combine cream cheese, crema, lime juice and remaining salt; spread over corn. Sprinkle with bread crumbs, jalapenos, chipotle powder and, if desired, cilantro.

NOTE This recipe was tested with Nestle crema; look for it in the international foods section.

NUTRITION FACTS 1 ear of corn: 339 cal., 26g fat (9g sat. fat), 39mg chol., 568mg sod., 25g carb. (8g sugars, 3g fiber), 6g pro.

Grilled Chicken, Mango & Blue Cheese Tortillas

Tortillas packed with chicken, mango and blue cheese make a fantastic appetizer to welcome summer. We double or triple the ingredients when we host parties.

—**JOSEE LANZI** NEW PORT RICHEY, FL

START TO FINISH: 30 MIN.
MAKES: 16 APPETIZERS

- 1 **boneless skinless chicken breast (8 ounces)**
- 1 **teaspoon blackened seasoning**
- ¾ **cup (6 ounces) plain yogurt**
- 1½ **teaspoons grated lime peel**
- 2 **tablespoons lime juice**
- ¼ **teaspoon salt**
- ⅛ **teaspoon pepper**
- 1 **cup finely chopped peeled mango**
- ⅓ **cup finely chopped red onion**
- 4 **flour tortillas (8 inches)**
- ½ **cup crumbled blue cheese**
- 2 **tablespoons minced fresh cilantro**

1. Lightly oil grill rack with cooking oil. Sprinkle chicken with blackened seasoning. Grill, covered, over medium heat 6-8 minutes on each side or until a thermometer reads 165°.

2. Meanwhile, in a small bowl, mix yogurt, lime peel, lime juice, salt and pepper. Cool the chicken slightly; finely chop and transfer to a small bowl. Stir in mango and onion.

3. Grill tortillas, uncovered, over medium heat 2-3 minutes or until puffed. Turn; top with chicken mixture and blue cheese. Grill, covered, 2-3 minutes longer or until bottoms of tortillas are lightly browned. Drizzle with yogurt mixture; sprinkle with cilantro. Cut each tortilla into four wedges.

NUTRITION FACTS 1 wedge: 85 cal., 3g fat (1g sat. fat), 12mg chol., 165mg sod., 10g carb. (2g sugars, 1g fiber), 5g pro. ***Diabetic Exchanges:*** 1 lean meat, ½ starch.

White Cheddar Mac & Cheese

My mac and cheese is simple and has lots of flavor from the cheeses and ground chipotle chile. I use conchiglie pasta because its large openings allow more melted cheese to pool inside. Yum!

—COLLEEN DELAWDER HERNDON, VA

START TO FINISH: 25 MIN.
MAKES: 8 SERVINGS

- 1 package (16 ounces) small pasta shells
- ½ cup butter, cubed
- ½ cup all-purpose flour
- ½ teaspoon onion powder
- ½ teaspoon ground chipotle pepper
- ½ teaspoon pepper
- ¼ teaspoon salt
- 4 cups 2% milk
- 2 cups shredded sharp white cheddar cheese
- 2 cups shredded Manchego or additional white cheddar cheese

1. In a 6-qt. stockpot, cook the pasta according to package directions. Drain; return to pot.

2. Meanwhile, in a large saucepan, melt butter over medium heat. Stir in flour and seasonings until smooth; gradually whisk in milk. Bring to a boil, stirring constantly; cook and stir until thickened, 6-8 minutes. Remove from heat; stir in cheeses until melted. Add to pasta; toss to coat.

NUTRITION FACTS 1 cup: 650 cal., 35g fat (22g sat. fat), 101mg chol., 607mg sod., 55g carb. (8g sugars, 2g fiber), 27g pro.

DID YOU KNOW?

The only difference between white and orange cheddar is the color. Orange cheddar gets its color from a plant additive that doesn't affect the flavor or texture. So feel free to use orange cheddar for this recipe if you prefer the appearance!

Southwest-Style Wedding Soup

I turned leftover hamburgers into meatballs and dreamed up this cozy southwestern soup. Now my Italian family asks for it over traditional wedding soup.
—**TEENA PETRUS** JOHNSTOWN, PA

START TO FINISH: 30 MIN.
MAKES: 6 SERVINGS

- 1 tablespoon canola oil
- 2 medium carrots, chopped
- 2 medium celery ribs, chopped
- ½ cup frozen corn, thawed
- 2 quarts chicken stock
- 1 cup soft bread crumbs
- 1 envelope reduced-sodium taco seasoning
- 1 large egg
- 1 pound ground chicken
- 1½ cups acini di pepe pasta
- 2 tablespoons minced fresh cilantro
- ¼ teaspoon salt
- Cubed avocado and sour cream

1. In a Dutch oven, heat oil over medium heat. Add carrots, celery and corn; cook until tender. Stir in stock. Increase heat to high; bring to a boil.

2. Meanwhile, combine bread crumbs, taco seasoning, egg and chicken; mix lightly. With wet hands, shape into 1½-in. balls. Reduce heat to simmer; gently drop meatballs into the stock. Cook, covered, until the meatballs are no longer pink, 8-10 minutes. Stir in pasta. Simmer, covered, until the pasta is tender, 6-8 minutes. Sprinkle with cilantro and salt. Serve with avocado and sour cream.

NOTE To make soft bread crumbs, tear bread into pieces and place in a food processor or blender. Cover and pulse until crumbs form. One slice of bread yields ½ to ¾ cup crumbs.

NUTRITION FACTS 1½ cups: 455 cal., 10g fat (2g sat. fat), 81mg chol., 1219mg sod., 63g carb. (8g sugars, 3g fiber), 29g pro.

Grilled Eggplant Sandwiches

This eggplant, tomato and goat cheese sandwich—grilled to perfection—makes a delicious meatless meal.

—JENNIFER JARAS CORONA, CA

START TO FINISH: 25 MIN.
MAKES: 2 SERVINGS

- **2 tablespoons olive oil**
- **1 garlic clove, minced**
- **2 ciabatta rolls, split**
- **4 slices eggplant (1/2 inch thick)**
- **1 medium heirloom tomato, cut into 1/2-inch slices**
- **1/4 teaspoon salt**
- **1/8 teaspoon pepper**
- **2 ounces fresh goat cheese, softened**
- **6 fresh basil leaves**

1. Mix oil and garlic; brush onto cut sides of rolls and both sides of vegetables. Sprinkle vegetables with salt and pepper.

2. Grill eggplant, covered, over medium heat, until tender, 4-5 minutes per side. Grill tomato, covered, until lightly browned, 1-2 minutes per side. Grill the rolls, cut side down, until toasted, 1-2 minutes.

3. Spread roll bottoms with goat cheese. Top with basil, eggplant and tomato; close sandwiches.

NOTE Make this hearty sandwich into a lower-calorie lunch or dinner by serving it open-face and using a knife and fork. You'll save more than 150 cal. per serving (and bring the sodium below 700mg).

NUTRITION FACTS 1 sandwich: 538 cal., 21g fat (5g sat. fat), 19mg chol., 958mg sod., 81g carb. (10g sugars, 7g fiber), 15g pro.

HOW TO

SOFTEN GOAT CHEESE

Goat cheese is naturally soft, but can be crumbly and hard to spread. To soften goat cheese to a spreading consistency, mash it with a spoonful or two of milk or cream. Or set it out for an hour and let it come to room temperature before using.

Vegetarian Pad Thai

This is a simple pad thai full of vegetables and flavor. It's quick, simple, and fresh.
—**COLLEEN DOUCETTE** TRURO, NS

START TO FINISH: 30 MIN.
MAKES: 4 SERVINGS

- **6 ounces uncooked thick rice noodles**
- **2 tablespoons packed brown sugar**
- **3 tablespoons reduced-sodium soy sauce**
- **4 teaspoons rice vinegar**
- **2 teaspoons lime juice**
- **2 teaspoons olive oil**
- **3 medium carrots, shredded**
- **1 medium sweet red pepper, cut into thin strips**
- **4 green onions, chopped**
- **3 garlic cloves, minced**
- **4 large eggs, lightly beaten**
- **2 cups bean sprouts**
- **1/3 cup chopped fresh cilantro**
- **Chopped peanuts, optional**
- **Lime wedges**

1. Prepare noodles according to the package directions. Drain; rinse well and drain again.

2. In a small bowl, mix together brown sugar, soy sauce, vinegar and lime juice. In a large nonstick skillet, heat oil over medium-high heat; stir-fry carrots and pepper until crisp-tender, 3-4 minutes. Add green onions and garlic; cook and stir 2 minutes. Remove from pan.

3. Reduce heat to medium. Pour eggs into the same pan; cook and stir until no liquid egg remains. Stir in the carrot mixture, noodles and sauce mixture; heat through. Add bean sprouts; toss to combine. Top with cilantro and, if desired, peanuts. Serve pad thai with lime wedges.

NUTRITION FACTS 1¼ cups: 339 cal., 8g fat (2g sat. fat), 186mg chol., 701mg sod., 55g carb. (15g sugars, 4g fiber), 12g pro.

Maple-Dijon Chicken

Eating dinner as a family every night is really important to us, and this recipe is one that we all love. It's our favorite skillet chicken dish.

—COURTNEY STULTZ WEIR, KS

START TO FINISH: 30 MIN.
MAKES: 4 SERVINGS

- **1 pound boneless skinless chicken breasts, cut into 1-inch-thick strips**
- **½ teaspoon dried rosemary, crushed**
- **½ teaspoon dried thyme**
- **½ teaspoon pepper**
- **¼ teaspoon salt**
- **1 tablespoon coconut oil or olive oil**
- **½ cup chopped onion**
- **1 garlic clove, minced**
- **⅓ cup Dijon mustard**
- **3 tablespoons maple syrup**

Toss chicken with seasonings. In a large skillet, heat oil over medium heat; saute chicken 10 minutes. Add onion and garlic; cook and stir for 5 minutes. Stir in mustard and syrup; cook and stir until sauce is caramelized and chicken is no longer pink, 5-7 minutes.

NUTRITION FACTS 1 serving: 221 cal., 6g fat (4g sat. fat), 63mg chol., 684mg sod., 13g carb. (10g sugars, 1g fiber), 23g pro. ***Diabetic Exchanges:*** 3 lean meat, 1 starch, ½ fat.

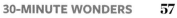

Pizza in a Bowl

On busy days, it's a comfort to know that my family can sit down to dinner minutes after we walk in the door. Double the recipe to wow a crowd at a potluck. This recipe works in a slow cooker, too.

—VIRGINIA KRITES CRIDERSVILLE, OH

START TO FINISH: 25 MIN.
MAKES: 6 SERVINGS

- **8 ounces uncooked rigatoni (about 3 cups)**
- **3/4 pound ground beef**
- **1/2 cup chopped onion**
- **1 can (15 ounces) pizza sauce**
- **2/3 cup condensed cream of mushroom soup, undiluted**
- **2 cups (8 ounces) shredded part-skim mozzarella cheese**
- **1 package (3 1/2 ounces) sliced pepperoni**
- **Chopped fresh basil or arugula, optional**

1. Cook rigatoni according to package directions; drain. Meanwhile, in a large skillet, cook beef and onion over medium heat 6-8 minutes or until beef is no longer pink, breaking up beef into crumbles; drain. Add pizza sauce, soup and cheese; cook and stir over low heat until the cheese is melted.

2. Add rigatoni and pepperoni to beef mixture. Heat mixture through, stirring to combine. If desired, top with basil before serving.

NUTRITION FACTS 1 cup: 495 cal., 25g fat (9g sat. fat), 74mg chol., 1056mg sod., 37g carb. (6g sugars, 3g fiber), 30g pro.

Greek Couscous Salad

I love the fresh taste of crisp veggies in a satisfying salad, hearty enough for a full meal.

—**TERI RASEY** CADILLAC, MI

PREP: 15 MIN. • **COOK:** 5 MIN. + COOLING
MAKES: 12 SERVINGS

- 1 can (14½ ounces) reduced-sodium chicken broth
- 1¾ cups uncooked whole wheat couscous (about 11 ounces)

DRESSING

- ½ cup olive oil
- 1½ teaspoons grated lemon peel
- ¼ cup lemon juice
- 1 teaspoon adobo seasoning
- ¼ teaspoon salt

SALAD

- 1 English cucumber, halved lengthwise and sliced
- 2 cups grape tomatoes, halved
- 1 cup coarsely chopped fresh parsley
- 1 can (6½ ounces) sliced ripe olives, drained
- 4 green onions, chopped
- ½ cup crumbled feta cheese

1. In a large saucepan, bring broth to a boil. Stir in couscous. Remove from heat; let stand, covered, until broth is absorbed, about 5 minutes. Transfer to a large bowl; cool completely.

2. Whisk together dressing ingredients. Add cucumber, tomatoes, parsley, olives and green onions to the couscous; stir in the dressing. Gently stir in the cheese. Serve immediately or refrigerate and serve cold.

NUTRITION FACTS ¾ cup: 335 cal., 18g fat (3g sat. fat), 4mg chol., 637mg sod., 39g carb. (3g sugars, 7g fiber), 9g pro.

DID YOU KNOW?

While English cucumbers are often also called "seedless cucumbers," they're not actually seedless. However, their seeds are tiny, so the cucumber is sweeter than the common ones we all know. Look for them in the produce section, sold in plastic wrap.

Italian Joes on Texas Toast

This is great for a weeknight on the go. If you double the crushed tomatoes, meat and wine, you'll have enough sauce to freeze.
—ASHLEY ARMSTRONG KINGSLAND, GA

START TO FINISH: 30 MIN.
MAKES: 8 SERVINGS

- 1 pound ground beef
- 1 small green pepper, finely chopped
- 1 medium onion, finely chopped
- 3 garlic cloves, minced
- ½ cup dry red wine or beef broth
- 1 can (14½ ounces) diced tomatoes, undrained
- ¼ cup tomato paste
- ¼ teaspoon salt
- ⅛ teaspoon pepper
- 1 package (11¼ ounces) frozen garlic Texas toast
- 8 slices part-skim mozzarella cheese

1. Preheat oven to 425°. In a large skillet, cook and crumble beef with green pepper, onion and garlic over medium-high heat until no longer pink, 5-7 minutes; drain. Stir in wine. Bring to a boil; cook until the wine is reduced by half, about 2 minutes. Stir in tomatoes, tomato paste, salt and pepper; return to a boil. Reduce heat; simmer, uncovered, until the mixture is thickened, for 2-3 minutes, stirring occasionally.

2. Meanwhile, place Texas toast on a foil-lined 15x10x1-in. pan; bake until lightly browned, 8-10 minutes.

3. Spoon beef mixture onto toasts; top with cheese. Bake until cheese is melted, 3-4 minutes. Serve immediately.

NUTRITION FACTS 1 open-faced sandwich: 353 cal., 19g fat (7g sat. fat), 58mg chol., 626mg sod., 25g carb. (5g sugars, 2g fiber), 22g pro.

Grilled Garden Pizza

Dazzle your family and friends with pizzas fresh off the grill. We top them with Asiago, Parmesan, veggies and fresh basil. Pile on the toppings you love.

—TERI RASEY CADILLAC, MI

START TO FINISH: 30 MIN.
MAKES: 6 SERVINGS

- **2 plum tomatoes, thinly sliced**
- **½ teaspoon sea salt or kosher salt**
- **1 loaf (1 pound) frozen pizza dough, thawed**
- **2 tablespoons olive oil, divided**
- **½ cup shredded Parmesan or Asiago cheese**
- **½ cup fresh or frozen corn, thawed**
- **¼ cup thinly sliced red onion**
- **8 ounces fresh mozzarella cheese, sliced**
- **½ cup thinly sliced fresh spinach**
- **3 tablespoons chopped fresh basil**

1. Sprinkle tomatoes with salt; set aside. On a lightly floured surface, divide dough in half. Roll or press each to ¼-in. thickness; place each on a greased sheet of foil (about 10 in. square). Brush tops with 1 tablespoon oil.

2. Carefully invert crusts onto a grill rack, removing foil. Brush tops with remaining oil. Grill, covered, over medium heat 2-3 minutes or until bottom is golden brown. Remove from grill; reduce grill temperature to low.

3. Top grilled sides of crusts with Parmesan or Asiago cheese, tomatoes, corn, onion and mozzarella cheese. Grill, covered, on low heat 4-6 minutes or until cheese is melted. Sprinkle with spinach and basil.

Fresh mozzarella has about the same cal. and fat as part-skim; they are both lighter than a lot of other cheeses like cheddar, Muenster and provolone.

NUTRITION FACTS 1 piece: 375 cal., 16g fat (7g sat. fat), 35mg chol., 680mg sod., 40g carb. (4g sugars, 1g fiber), 15g pro.

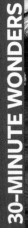

Cilantro Lime Shrimp

A quick garlicky lime marinade works magic on these juicy shrimp. They come off the grill with huge flavors that are perfect for your next cookout.

—**MELISSA RODRIGUEZ** VAN NUYS, CA

START TO FINISH: 30 MIN.
MAKES: 4 SERVINGS

- 1/3 cup chopped fresh cilantro
- 1 1/2 teaspoons grated lime peel
- 1/3 cup lime juice
- 1 jalapeno pepper, seeded and minced
- 2 tablespoons olive oil
- 3 garlic cloves, minced
- 1/4 teaspoon salt
- 1/4 teaspoon ground cumin
- 1/4 teaspoon pepper
- 1 pound uncooked shrimp (16-20 per pound), peeled and deveined
- Lime slices

1. Mix the first nine ingredients; toss with shrimp. Let stand 15 minutes.

2. Thread shrimp and lime slices onto four metal or soaked wooden skewers. Grill, covered, over medium heat until shrimp turn pink, 2-4 minutes per side.

NUTRITION FACTS 1 kabob: 167 cal., 8g fat (1g sat. fat), 138mg chol., 284mg sod., 4g carb. (1g sugars, 0 fiber), 19g pro. ***Diabetic Exchanges:*** 3 lean meat, 1 1/2 fat.

TOP TIP

Soaking wooden skewers for 30 minutes prior to loading them and putting them on the grill helps prevent the wood from charring or burning. Metal skewers don't need to be soaked, but do get very hot on the grill and should be handled with care.

Bucatini with Sausage & Kale, p. 74

CHAPTER 3

5-INGREDIENT ENTREES

Save time and money with these delicious main courses!

Pierogi Chicken Supper 70

Pork Chops with Honey-Garlic Sauce 73

Bucatini with Sausage & Kale 74

Grilled Tilapia Piccata 77

Grilled Flank Steak 78

Artichoke Blue Cheese Fettuccine 81

Zesty Grilled Ham 82

Lemon-Parsley Tilapia 85

Bacon-Wrapped Pesto Pork Tenderloin 86

Bacon & Cheddar Chicken 89

Savory Beer Pork Chops 90

Grilled Basil Chicken & Tomatoes 93

Apple-Glazed Chicken Thighs 94

Tortellini Carbonara 97

5 INGREDIENTS

Pierogi Chicken Supper

This change-of-pace dish combines chicken, cheese and onion with frozen pierogies for a complete meal in just 30 minutes.
—**BARBARA SCOTT** WALKERSVILLE, MD

START TO FINISH: 30 MIN.
MAKES: 4 SERVINGS

- **1 package (16 ounces) frozen pierogies**
- **1 pound boneless skinless chicken breasts, cut into 2x½-inch strips**
- **¼ teaspoon salt**
- **⅛ teaspoon pepper**
- **2 tablespoons butter, divided**
- **½ large sweet onion, thinly sliced**
- **½ cup shredded cheddar cheese**

1. Cook pierogies according to package directions; drain. Meanwhile, toss chicken with salt and pepper. In a large nonstick skillet, heat 1 tablespoon butter over medium-high heat; saute chicken and onion until the chicken is no longer pink. Remove from pan.

2. In same pan, heat remaining butter over medium heat; saute pierogies until lightly browned. Stir in chicken mixture; sprinkle with cheese. Cover; remove from heat and let stand until the cheese is melted.

NUTRITION FACTS 1 cup: 444 cal., 16g fat (8g sat. fat), 101mg chol., 762mg sod., 40g carb. (10g sugars, 3g fiber), 33g pro.

5 INGREDIENTS

Pork Chops with Honey-Garlic Sauce

The honey and garlic sauce is so good, I sometimes double it so there's extra for dipping.
—**MICHELLE SMITH** ELDERSBURG, MD

START TO FINISH: 25 MIN.
MAKES: 4 SERVINGS

- **4 bone-in pork loin chops (6 ounces each)**
- **¼ cup lemon juice**
- **¼ cup honey**
- **2 tablespoons reduced-sodium soy sauce**
- **1 garlic clove, minced**

In a large nonstick skillet coated with cooking spray, cook pork chops over medium heat until a thermometer reads 145°, 5-6 minutes on each side. Remove; let stand for 5 minutes. Combine the remaining ingredients; add to pan. Cook over medium heat 3-4 minutes, stirring occasionally. Serve with chops.

NUTRITION FACTS 1 pork chop with 2 tablespoons sauce: 249 cal., 7g fat (3g sat. fat), 74mg chol., 342mg sod., 19g carb. (18g sugars, 0 fiber), 27g pro. ***Diabetic Exchanges:*** 4 lean meat, 1 starch.

5 INGREDIENTS

Bucatini with Sausage & Kale

I was short on time but wanted to make an elegant dinner for my husband and me. That night, we ate this simple pasta starring spicy sausage and our homegrown kale.
—ANGELA LEMOINE HOWELL, NJ

START TO FINISH: 30 MIN.
MAKES: 6 SERVINGS

1 package (12 ounces) bucatini pasta or fettuccine
2 teaspoons plus 3 tablespoons olive oil, divided
1 pound regular or spicy bulk Italian sausage
5 garlic cloves, thinly sliced
8 cups chopped fresh kale (about 5 ounces)
¾ teaspoon salt
¼ teaspoon pepper
Shredded Romano cheese

1. Cook pasta according to the package directions, decreasing time by 3 minutes. Drain, reserving 2 cups pasta water. Toss pasta with 2 teaspoons oil.

2. In a 6-qt. stockpot, cook sausage over medium heat until no longer pink, 5-7 minutes, breaking sausage into large crumbles. Add garlic and remaining oil; cook and stir 2 minutes. Stir in kale, salt and pepper; cook, covered, over medium-low heat until kale is tender, about 10 minutes, stirring occasionally.

3. Add pasta and the reserved pasta water; bring to a boil. Reduce heat; simmer, uncovered, the until pasta is al dente and the liquid is absorbed, about 3 minutes, tossing to combine. Sprinkle with cheese.

NUTRITION FACTS 1⅓ cups: 512 cal., 30g fat (8g sat. fat), 51mg chol., 898mg sod., 43g carb. (2g sugars, 3g fiber), 19g pro.

5 INGREDIENTS

Grilled Tilapia Piccata

We aren't big fish eaters, but when a friend made this for us, we couldn't believe how wonderful it was! Now we eat it regularly. I love making it for guests—it's simple, looks lovely and tastes restaurant-worthy.
—**BETH COOPER** COLUMBUS, OH

START TO FINISH: 25 MIN.
MAKES: 4 SERVINGS

- ½ teaspoon grated lemon peel
- 3 tablespoons lemon juice
- 2 tablespoons olive oil
- 2 garlic cloves, minced
- 2 teaspoons capers, drained
- 3 tablespoons minced fresh basil, divided
- 4 tilapia fillets (6 ounces each)
- ½ teaspoon salt
- ¼ teaspoon pepper

1. In a small bowl, whisk lemon peel, lemon juice, oil and garlic until blended; stir in capers and 2 tablespoons basil. Reserve 2 tablespoons of the mixture for drizzling cooked fish. Brush the remaining mixture onto both sides of tilapia; sprinkle with salt and pepper.

2. On a lightly oiled grill rack, grill tilapia, covered, over medium heat, or broil 4 in. from heat 3-4 minutes on each side or until fish just begins to flake easily with a fork. Drizzle with the reserved lemon mixture; sprinkle with remaining basil.

NOTE Look for U.S. or Canadian tilapia that's been farmed in closed tanks for the least impact on the environment.

NUTRITION FACTS 1 fillet: 206 cal., 8g fat (2g sat. fat), 83mg chol., 398mg sod., 2g carb. (0 sugars, 0 fiber), 32g pro. ***Diabetic Exchanges:*** 5 lean meat, 1½ fat.

(5) INGREDIENTS

Grilled Flank Steak

The marinade for this steak only requires four ingredients, but that's not why it will be your new favorite dinner. The flavors are spot on, and the meat turns out fork-tender every time. If you don't have a grill, you can easily broil the steaks instead.

—HEATHER AHRENS COLUMBUS, OH

PREP: 10 MIN. + MARINATING
COOK: 20 MIN.
MAKES: 6 SERVINGS

- **1 cup reduced-sodium soy sauce**
- **1/4 cup lemon juice**
- **1/4 cup honey**
- **6 garlic cloves, minced**
- **1 beef flank steak (1 1/2 pounds)**

1. In a large resealable plastic bag, combine soy sauce, lemon juice, honey and garlic; add steak. Seal bag and turn to coat; refrigerate for 6-8 hours.

2. Drain and discard marinade. Broil 4-6 in. from the heat or grill over medium heat for 8-10 minutes on each side or until the meat reaches desired doneness (for medium-rare, a thermometer should read 135°; medium, 140°; medium-well, 145°). Thinly slice the steak across the grain.

NUTRITION FACTS 3 ounces cooked beef: 186 cal., 8g fat (4g sat. fat), 54mg chol., 471mg sod., 4g carb. (3g sugars, 0 fiber), 23g pro. ***Diabetic Exchanges:*** 3 lean meat.

(5) INGREDIENTS

Artichoke Blue Cheese Fettuccine

When I'm in a rush, I use store-bought Alfredo sauce to speed along these blue-cheesy noodles with mushrooms. Fresh refrigerated fettuccine can get this dish done even faster.

—JOLANTHE ERB HARRISONBURG, VA

START TO FINISH: 20 MIN.
MAKES: 4 SERVINGS

- **1 package (12 ounces) fettuccine**
- **1 cup sliced fresh mushrooms**
- **1 can (14 ounces) water-packed artichoke hearts, drained and chopped**
- **1½ cups Alfredo sauce**
- **¼ cup crumbled blue cheese**

1. Cook fettuccine according to package directions. Drain, reserving ⅓ cup pasta water.

2. While the pasta is cooking, coat a large nonstick skillet with cooking spray. Cook and stir the mushrooms and artichoke hearts over medium heat until mushrooms are tender. Stir in Alfredo sauce; bring to a boil. Reduce heat; simmer, uncovered, 5 minutes, stirring occasionally.

3. Add fettuccine to artichoke mixture; toss to combine, adding reserved pasta water if desired. Sprinkle with crumbled blue cheese.

NUTRITION FACTS 1 cup: 499 cal., 14g fat (9g sat. fat), 33mg chol., 770mg sod., 74g carb. (6g sugars, 4g fiber), 21g pro.

5 INGREDIENTS

Zesty Grilled Ham

If it's ham, my kids will eat it, and they like this kicked-up recipe best of all. Even the small ones eat adult-sized portions, so be sure to make plenty.
—MARY ANN LIEN TYLER, TX

START TO FINISH: 15 MIN.
MAKES: 4 SERVINGS

- **1/3 cup packed brown sugar**
- **2 tablespoons prepared horseradish**
- **4 teaspoons lemon juice**
- **1 fully cooked bone-in ham steak (1 pound)**

1. Place brown sugar, horseradish and lemon juice in a small saucepan; bring to a boil, stirring constantly. Brush over both sides of ham.

2. Place ham on an oiled grill rack over medium heat. Grill, covered, until glazed and heated through, 7-10 minutes, turning occasionally.

NUTRITION FACTS 1 serving: 180 cal., 5g fat (2g sat. fat), 44mg chol., 845mg sod., 20g carb. (19g sugars, 0 fiber), 14g pro.

5 INGREDIENTS

Lemon-Parsley Tilapia

I like to include seafood in our weekly dinner rotation but don't want to bother with anything complicated (and it had better taste good or the family will riot). This herbed fish does the trick.

—**TRISHA KRUSE** EAGLE, ID

START TO FINISH: 20 MIN.
MAKES: 4 SERVINGS

- **4 tilapia fillets (about 4 ounces each)**
- **2 tablespoons lemon juice**
- **1 tablespoon butter, melted**
- **2 tablespoons minced fresh parsley**
- **2 garlic cloves, minced**
- **2 teaspoons grated lemon peel**
- **½ teaspoon salt**
- **¼ teaspoon pepper**

1. Preheat oven to 375°. Place the tilapia in a parchment paper-lined 15x10x1-in. pan. Drizzle with lemon juice, then melted butter.

2. Bake until fish just begins to flake easily with a fork, 11-13 minutes. Meanwhile, mix remaining ingredients. Remove fish from oven; sprinkle with parsley mixture.

NUTRITION FACTS 1 fillet: 124 cal., 4g fat (2g sat. fat), 63mg chol., 359mg sod., 1g carb. (0 sugars, 0 fiber), 21g pro. ***Diabetic Exchanges:*** 3 lean meat, 1 fat.

5 INGREDIENTS

Bacon-Wrapped Pesto Pork Tenderloin

I love to serve this family-favorite tenderloin—maybe because of the compliments that come with it! When the weather warms up, we grill it.
—MEGAN RIOFSKI FRANKFORT, IL

PREP: 30 MIN. • **BAKE:** 20 MIN.
MAKES: 4 SERVINGS

- **10 bacon strips**
- **1 pork tenderloin (1 pound)**
- **1/4 teaspoon pepper**
- **1/3 cup prepared pesto**
- **1 cup shredded Italian cheese blend**
- **1 cup fresh baby spinach**

1. Preheat oven to 425°. Arrange bacon strips lengthwise in a foil-lined 15x10x1-in. pan, overlapping slightly.

2. Cut tenderloin lengthwise through the center to within 1/2 in. of bottom. Open tenderloin flat; cover with plastic wrap. Pound with a meat mallet to 1/2-in. thickness. Remove the plastic; place tenderloin on the center of the bacon, perpendicular to strips.

3. Sprinkle pepper over pork. Spread with pesto; layer with cheese and spinach. Close tenderloin; wrap with bacon, overlapping ends. Tie with kitchen string at 3-in. intervals. Secure ends with toothpicks.

4. In a 12-in. skillet, brown roast on all sides, about 8 minutes. Return to baking pan; roast until a thermometer inserted in the pork reads 145°, 17-20 minutes. Remove string and toothpicks; let stand 5 minutes before slicing.

NUTRITION FACTS 1 serving: 402 cal., 25g fat (9g sat. fat), 104mg chol., 864mg sod., 4g carb. (1g sugars, 1g fiber), 37g pro.

5 INGREDIENTS

Bacon & Cheddar Chicken

Cheese and bacon don't usually come light. But this tasty recipe keeps the fat and calories low and flavor high. This family-friendly recipe can easily be doubled to serve a larger group.

—TRISHA KRUSE EAGLE, ID

START TO FINISH: 30 MIN.
MAKES: 4 SERVINGS

- **4 bacon strips, chopped**
- **4 boneless skinless chicken breast halves (6 ounces each)**
- **1/4 teaspoon salt**
- **1/4 teaspoon pepper**
- **2/3 cup barbecue sauce, divided**
- **1/2 cup shredded cheddar cheese**
- **Thinly sliced green onions**

1. Preheat oven to 350°. In an ovenproof skillet, cook bacon over medium heat until crisp, stirring occasionally. Using a slotted spoon, remove bacon to paper towels; reserve drippings.

2. Sprinkle chicken with salt and pepper. In same pan, brown chicken in drippings over medium heat, 3-4 minutes per side. Brush with 1/3 cup of barbecue sauce Transfer to oven; bake 8 minutes.

3. Spoon the remaining sauce over the chicken; sprinkle with cheese and bacon. Bake until the cheese is melted and a thermometer reads 165°, 4-6 minutes. Sprinkle with green onions.

NUTRITION FACTS 1 chicken breast half: 435 cal., 20g fat (8g sat. fat), 126mg chol., 973mg sod., 19g carb. (15g sugars, 0 fiber), 41g pro.

TOP TIP

I recently tried a recipe that called for 3/4 cup green onions. Instead of using a knife, I found that snipping the onions with a pair of kitchen scissors or shears took only a few seconds.

—Kristy B., Kelowna, British Columbia

5 INGREDIENTS

Savory Beer Pork Chops

These tender chops in savory sauce are perfect for a hectic weeknight because they're so easy to prep. They use only five ingredients! Try them with hot buttery noodles.

—JANA CHRISTIAN FARSON, WY

START TO FINISH: 20 MIN.
MAKES: 4 SERVINGS

- **4 boneless pork loin chops (4 ounces each)**
- **1/2 teaspoon salt**
- **1/2 teaspoon pepper**
- **1 tablespoon canola oil**
- **3 tablespoons ketchup**
- **2 tablespoons brown sugar**
- **3/4 cup beer or nonalcoholic beer**

1. Sprinkle pork chops with salt and pepper. In a large skillet, heat oil over medium heat; brown chops on both sides.

2. Mix ketchup, brown sugar and beer; pour over chops. Bring to a boil. Reduce heat; simmer, uncovered, until a thermometer inserted in pork reads 145°, 4-6 minutes. Let stand 5 minutes before serving.

NUTRITION FACTS 1 pork chop: 239 cal., 10g fat (3g sat. fat), 55mg chol., 472mg sod., 11g carb. (11g sugars, 0 fiber), 22g pro. ***Diabetic Exchanges:*** 3 lean meat, 1 fat, 1/2 starch.

5 INGREDIENTS

Grilled Basil Chicken & Tomatoes

Relax after work with a cold drink while this savory chicken marinates in an herby tomato blend for an hour, then toss it on the grill. It tastes just like summer.
—LAURA LUNARDI WEST CHESTER, PA

PREP: 15 MIN. + MARINATING
GRILL: 10 MIN.
MAKES: 4 SERVINGS

- **3/4 cup balsamic vinegar**
- **1/4 cup tightly packed fresh basil leaves**
- **2 tablespoons olive oil**
- **1 garlic clove, minced**
- **1/2 teaspoon salt**
- **8 plum tomatoes**
- **4 boneless skinless chicken breast halves (4 ounces each)**

1. For the marinade, place the first five ingredients in a blender. Cut four of the tomatoes into quarters and add to blender; cover and process until blended. Halve the remaining tomatoes for grilling.

2. In a bowl, combine chicken and 2/3 cup marinade; refrigerate, covered, 1 hour, turning occasionally. Reserve remaining marinade for serving.

3. Place chicken on an oiled grill rack over medium heat; discard marinade remaining in bowl. Grill chicken, covered, until a thermometer reads 165°, 4-6 minutes per side. Grill tomatoes, covered, over medium heat until lightly browned, 2-4 minutes per side. Serve chicken and tomatoes with reserved marinade.

NUTRITION FACTS 1 serving: 177 cal., 5g fat (1g sat. fat), 63mg chol., 171mg sod., 8g carb. (7g sugars, 1g fiber), 24g pro. ***Diabetic Exchanges:*** 3 lean meat, 1 vegetable, 1/2 fat.

HOW TO

MINCE & CHOP

1. Hold the handle of a chef's knife in one hand; rest the fingers of your other hand on the top of the blade near the tip. Using the handle to guide and apply pressure, move knife in an arc across the food with a rocking motion.
2. Mincing results in pieces 1/8 in. or smaller; chopping produces 1/4-in. to 1/2-in. pieces.

(5) INGREDIENTS

Apple-Glazed Chicken Thighs

My pickatarian-child is choosy but willing to eat this chicken glazed with apple juice and thyme. I dish it up with mashed potatoes and green beans.

—**KERRY PICARD** SPOKANE, WA

START TO FINISH: 25 MIN.
MAKES: 6 SERVINGS

- **6 boneless skinless chicken thighs (1½ pounds)**
- **¾ teaspoon seasoned salt**
- **¼ teaspoon pepper**
- **1 tablespoon canola oil**
- **1 cup unsweetened apple juice**
- **1 teaspoon minced fresh thyme or ¼ teaspoon dried thyme**

1. Sprinkle chicken with seasoned salt and pepper. In a large skillet, heat oil over medium-high heat. Brown chicken on both sides. Remove from pan.

2. Add juice and thyme to skillet. Bring to a boil, stirring to loosen browned bits from pan; cook until liquid is reduced by half. Return chicken to pan; cook, covered, over medium heat 3-4 minutes longer or until a thermometer inserted in chicken reads 170°.

NUTRITION FACTS 1 chicken thigh with about 1 tablespoon glaze: 204 cal., 11g fat (2g sat. fat), 76mg chol., 255mg sod., 5g carb. (4g sugars, 0 fiber), 21g pro. ***Diabetic Exchanges:*** 3 lean meat, ½ fat.

5 INGREDIENTS

Tortellini Carbonara

Bacon, cream and Parmesan cheese make a classic pasta sauce that's absolutely heavenly. It's a great option for company!

—**CATHY CROYLE** DAVIDSVILLE, PA

START TO FINISH: 20 MIN.
MAKES: 4 SERVINGS

- **1 package (9 ounces) refrigerated cheese tortellini**
- **8 bacon strips, chopped**
- **1 cup heavy whipping cream**
- **½ cup grated Parmesan cheese**
- **½ cup chopped fresh parsley**

1. Cook tortellini according to package directions; drain.

2. Meanwhile, in a large skillet, cook bacon over medium heat until crisp, stirring occasionally. Remove with a slotted spoon; drain on paper towels. Pour off drippings.

3. In same pan, combine cream, cheese, parsley and bacon; heat through over medium heat. Stir in tortellini. Serve immediately.

NUTRITION FACTS 1 cup: 527 cal., 36g fat (20g sat. fat), 121mg chol., 728mg sod., 33g carb. (3g sugars, 2g fiber), 19g pro.

Spicy Peanut Chicken & Noodles, **p. 119**

CHAPTER 4

MEAL-IN-ONE MAINSTAYS

Menu planning is a snap with comforting one-dish entrees.

Sausage-Stuffed Butternut Squash. . 100
Penne & Smoked Sausage 103
Rosemary Shrimp with Spaghetti . . . 104
Spaghetti Squash
Meatball Casserole 107
Asian Chicken Rice Bowl 108
Asparagus Beef Lo Mein 111
One-Pan Tuscan Ravioli 112
Lemony Chicken & Rice 115
Taco Noodle Dish 116
Spicy Peanut Chicken & Noodles. . . . 119
Skillet Ham & Rice 120
Spicy Cajun Sausage & Rice Skillet. . . .123
Chicken Enchilada Bake 124
Garlic Shrimp & Rice Salad. 127
Tandoori Chicken Pita Pizzas 128

⑤ INGREDIENTS

Sausage-Stuffed Butternut Squash

Load butternut squash shells with an Italian turkey sausage and squash mixture for a quick and easy meal. Even better, it's good, and surprisingly low in calories.
—**KATIA SLINGER** WEST JORDAN, UT

START TO FINISH: 30 MIN.
MAKES: 4 SERVINGS

- **1 medium butternut squash (about 3 pounds)**
- **1 pound Italian turkey sausage links, casings removed**
- **1 medium onion, finely chopped**
- **4 garlic cloves, minced**
- **½ cup shredded Italian cheese blend**
- **Crushed red pepper flakes, optional**

1. Preheat broiler. Cut squash lengthwise in half; discard seeds. Place squash in a large microwave-safe dish, cut side down; add ½ in. of water. Microwave, covered, on high until soft, 20-25 minutes. Cool squash slightly.

2. Meanwhile, in a large nonstick skillet, cook and crumble sausage with onion over medium-high heat until no longer pink, 5-7 minutes. Add garlic; cook and stir 1 minute.

3. Leaving ½-in.-thick shells, scoop pulp from squash and stir into the sausage mixture. Place squash shells on a baking sheet; fill with sausage mixture. Sprinkle with cheese.

4. Broil 4-5 in. from heat until cheese is melted, 1-2 minutes. If desired, sprinkle with pepper flakes. To serve, cut each half into two portions.

NUTRITION FACTS 1 serving: 325 cal., 10g fat (4g sat. fat), 52mg chol., 587mg sod., 44g carb. (10g sugars, 12g fiber), 19g pro. ***Diabetic Exchanges:*** 3 starch, 3 lean meat.

TOP TIP

Butternut squash is an excellent source of vitamin A in the form of beta-carotene. It's important for normal vision and a healthy immune system, and it helps the heart, lungs and kidneys function properly.

FREEZE IT

Penne & Smoked Sausage

My sausage-pasta dish is a must-try. It just tastes so good when it's hot and bubbly from the oven! The cheddar french-fried onions lend a cheesy, crunchy touch.

—**MARGARET WILSON** SAN BERNARDINO, CA

PREP: 15 MIN. • **BAKE:** 30 MIN.
MAKES: 6 SERVINGS

- **2 cups uncooked penne pasta**
- **1 pound smoked sausage, cut into ¼-inch slices**
- **1½ cups 2% milk**
- **1 can (10¾ ounces) condensed cream of celery soup, undiluted**
- **1½ cups cheddar french-fried onions, divided**
- **1 cup shredded part-skim mozzarella cheese, divided**
- **1 cup frozen peas**

1. Preheat oven to 375°. Cook pasta according to package directions.

2. Meanwhile, in a large skillet, brown sausage over medium heat 5 minutes; drain. In a large bowl, combine milk and soup. Stir in ½ cup onions, ½ cup cheese, peas and sausage. Drain pasta; stir into the sausage mixture.

3. Transfer to a greased 13x9-in. baking dish. Cover and bake 25-30 minutes or until bubbly. Sprinkle with remaining onions and cheese. Bake, uncovered, for 3-5 minutes longer or until the cheese is melted.

FREEZE OPTION Sprinkle remaining onions and cheese over the unbaked casserole. Cover and freeze. To use, partially thaw in refrigerator overnight. Remove from refrigerator 30 minutes before baking. Preheat oven to 375°. Bake casserole as directed, increasing time as necessary to heat through and for a thermometer inserted in center to read 165°.

NUTRITION FACTS 1½ cups: 553 cal., 35g fat (14g sat. fat), 70mg chol., 1425mg sod., 36g carb. (7g sugars, 3g fiber), 22g pro.

Rosemary Shrimp with Spaghetti

I came up with this recipe on a busy night during the week when I was pressed for time. Now it's my go-to dish whenever I need a quick, nutritious meal. Serve this with garlic bread so you can scoop every last bit of goodness off your plate!

—**CANDACE HAVELY** STERLING, CO

START TO FINISH: 30 MIN.
MAKES: 4 SERVINGS

- **8 ounces uncooked white fiber or whole wheat spaghetti**
- **1 tablespoon olive oil**
- **1 pound uncooked shrimp (31-40 per pound), peeled and deveined**
- **2 garlic cloves, minced**
- **1½ teaspoons minced fresh rosemary or ½ teaspoon dried rosemary, crushed**
- **2 cups fresh baby spinach**
- **2 tablespoons lemon juice**
- **¼ teaspoon salt**
- **¼ teaspoon pepper**
- **¼ cup crumbled feta cheese**

1. Cook spaghetti according to package directions. Drain, reserving ½ cup of the pasta water.

2. Meanwhile, in a large skillet, heat oil over medium heat. Add shrimp, garlic and rosemary; cook and stir 3-4 minutes or just until the shrimp turn pink. Stir in the spinach; cook, covered, until slightly wilted.

3. Add spaghetti, lemon juice, salt and pepper; toss to combine, adding reserved pasta water as desired. Sprinkle with cheese. Remove from heat; let stand, covered, until the cheese is softened.

NUTRITION FACTS 1½ cups: 349 cal., 7g fat (2g sat. fat), 142mg chol., 366mg sod., 46g carb. (2g sugars, 8g fiber), 29g pro. ***Diabetic Exchanges:*** 3 starch, 3 lean meat, ½ fat.

Spaghetti Squash Meatball Casserole

One of our favorite comfort food dinners is spaghetti and meatballs. We really love this lightened up, healthier version that features extra veggies. You get the same great flavors with more nutrition!
—**COURTNEY STULTZ** WEIR, KS

PREP: 35 MIN. • **BAKE:** 30 MIN.
MAKES: 6 SERVINGS

- 1 medium spaghetti squash (about 4 pounds)
- ½ teaspoon salt, divided
- ½ teaspoon fennel seed
- ¼ teaspoon ground coriander
- ¼ teaspoon dried basil
- ¼ teaspoon dried oregano
- 1 pound lean ground beef (90% lean)
- 2 teaspoons olive oil
- 1 medium onion, chopped
- 1 garlic clove, minced
- 2 cups chopped collard greens
- 1 cup chopped fresh spinach
- 1 cup reduced-fat ricotta cheese
- 2 plum tomatoes, chopped
- 1 cup pasta sauce
- 1 cup shredded part-skim mozzarella cheese

1. Preheat oven to 350°. Cut squash lengthwise in half; discard the seeds. Place halves on a microwave-safe plate, cut side down. Microwave, uncovered, on high until tender, 15-20 minutes. Cool slightly.

2. Mix ¼ teaspoon salt with remaining seasonings; add to beef, mixing lightly but thoroughly. Shape into 1½-in. balls. In a large skillet, brown meatballs over medium heat; remove from pan.

3. In same pan, heat oil over medium heat; saute onion until tender, 3-4 minutes. Add garlic; cook and stir for 1 minute. Stir in the collard greens, spinach, ricotta cheese and remaining salt; remove from heat.

4. Using a fork, separate the strands of spaghetti squash; stir into the greens mixture. Transfer to a greased 13x9-in. baking dish. Top with tomatoes, meatballs, sauce and cheese. Bake, uncovered, until the meatballs are cooked through, 30-35 minutes.

NUTRITION FACTS 1 serving: 362 cal., 16g fat (6g sat. fat), 69mg chol., 618mg sod., 32g carb. (7g sugars, 7g fiber), 26g pro. ***Diabetic Exchanges:*** 3 lean meat, 2 starch, 1 fat.

Asian Chicken Rice Bowl

This super flavorful, nutrient-packed dish makes use of supermarket conveniences like coleslaw mix and rotisserie chicken. The recipe is easily doubled or tripled for large families.

—**CHRISTIANNA GOZZI** ASTORIA, NY

START TO FINISH: 20 MIN.
MAKES: 4 SERVINGS

- ¼ cup rice vinegar
- 1 green onion, minced
- 2 tablespoons reduced-sodium soy sauce
- 1 tablespoon toasted sesame seeds
- 1 tablespoon sesame oil
- 1 tablespoon honey
- 1 teaspoon minced fresh gingerroot
- 1 package (8.8 ounces) ready-to-serve brown rice
- 4 cups coleslaw mix (about 9 ounces)
- 2 cups shredded rotisserie chicken, chilled
- 2 cups frozen shelled edamame, thawed

1. For dressing, whisk together the first seven ingredients. Cook rice according to the package directions. Divide among four bowls.

2. In a large bowl, toss coleslaw mix and chicken with half of the dressing. Serve edamame and slaw mixture over rice; drizzle with remaining dressing.

NUTRITION FACTS 1 serving: 429 cal., 15g fat (2g sat. fat), 62mg chol., 616mg sod., 38g carb. (13g sugars, 5g fiber), 32g pro. ***Diabetic Exchanges:*** 3 lean meat, 2 starch, 1 vegetable, 1 fat.

TOP TIP

When buying fresh gingerroot, look for a smooth skin. If it's wrinkled and cracked, the root is dry and past its prime. Unpeeled gingerroot can be frozen in a heavy-duty resealable plastic bag for up to 1 year. When needed, simply peel and grate.

(5) INGREDIENTS

Asparagus Beef Lo Mein

This springtime beef stir-fry is as easy as it gets. Ramen noodles make it extra fun.
—**DOTTIE WANAT** MODESTO, CA

START TO FINISH: 20 MIN.
MAKES: 4 SERVINGS

- **1 beef top sirloin steak (1 pound), cut into thin strips**
- **2 packages (3 ounces each) beef ramen noodles**
- **⅔ cup hoisin sauce**
- **2¼ cups water, divided**
- **2 tablespoons olive oil, divided**
- **1 pound fresh asparagus, trimmed and cut into 2½-inch pieces**
- **1 small garlic clove, minced**

1. Toss beef with ½ teaspoon of seasoning from one of the ramen seasoning packets (discard the remaining opened packet). In a small bowl, mix hoisin sauce and ¼ cup water.

2. In a saucepan, bring the remaining water to a boil. Add the noodles and contents of the unopened seasoning packet; cook, uncovered, for 3 minutes. Remove from heat; let stand, covered, until the noodles are tender.

3. Meanwhile, in a large skillet, heat 1 tablespoon oil over medium-high heat; stir-fry beef until browned, 3-4 minutes. Remove from pan.

4. In same pan, heat the remaining oil over medium-high heat; stir-fry the asparagus with garlic until crisp-tender, 1-3 minutes. Stir in the hoisin sauce mixture; bring to a boil. Cook until slightly thickened. Stir in beef; heat through. Serve over noodles.

NUTRITION FACTS 1 serving: 511 cal., 21g fat (7g sat. fat), 47mg chol., 1367mg sod., 48g carb. (13g sugars, 3g fiber), 31g pro.

One-Pan Tuscan Ravioli

This recipe is very flexible, depending on what ingredients you have on hand. Sometimes I use chickpeas instead of cannellini beans for this recipe, grated Asiago or Provolone instead of Parmesan, and all zucchini if I don't have eggplant.
—**SONYA LABBE** WEST HOLLYWOOD, CA

START TO FINISH: 25 MIN.
MAKES: 4 SERVINGS

1 tablespoon olive oil
2 cups cubed eggplant (1/2 inch)
1 can (14 1/2 ounces) Italian diced tomatoes, undrained
1 can (14 1/2 ounces) reduced-sodium chicken broth
1 medium zucchini, halved lengthwise and cut into 1/2-inch slices
1 package (9 ounces) refrigerated cheese ravioli
1 can (15 ounces) cannellini beans, rinsed and drained
Shredded Parmesan cheese
Thinly sliced fresh basil

1. In a large skillet, heat oil over medium heat; saute eggplant until lightly browned, 2-3 minutes.

2. Stir in tomatoes, broth and zucchini; bring to a boil. Add ravioli; cook, uncovered, over medium heat until ravioli are tender, 7-9 minutes, stirring occasionally. Stir in beans; heat through. Sprinkle with cheese and basil.

NUTRITION FACTS 1 1/2 cups: 376 cal., 10g fat (4g sat. fat), 36mg chol., 1096mg sod., 56g carb. (11g sugars, 8g fiber), 16g pro.

Lemony Chicken & Rice

I couldn't say who loves this recipe best, because every time I serve it, it gets raves! Occasionally I even get a phone call or email from a friend requesting the recipe, and it's certainly a favorite of my grown children and 15 grandchildren.

—**MARYALICE WOOD** LANGLEY, BC

PREP: 15 MIN. + MARINATING
BAKE: 55 MIN.
MAKES: 2 CASSEROLES (4 SERVINGS EACH)

- 2 cups water
- 1/2 cup reduced-sodium soy sauce
- 1/4 cup lemon juice
- 1/4 cup olive oil
- 2 garlic cloves, minced
- 2 teaspoons ground ginger
- 2 teaspoons pepper
- 16 bone-in chicken thighs, skin removed (about 6 pounds)
- 2 cups uncooked long grain rice
- 4 tablespoons grated lemon peel, divided
- 2 medium lemons, sliced

1. In a large resealable plastic bag, combine the first seven ingredients. Add chicken; seal bag and turn to coat. Refrigerate 4 hours or overnight.

2. Preheat oven to 325°. Spread 1 cup rice into each of two greased 13x9-in. baking dishes. Top each with 1 tablespoon lemon peel, 8 chicken thighs and half of the marinade. Top with sliced lemons.

3. Bake, covered, for 40 minutes. Uncover; bake 15-20 minutes longer or until a thermometer inserted in chicken reads 170-175°. Sprinkle with the remaining lemon peel.

NUTRITION FACTS 2 chicken thighs with 3/4 cup rice mixture: 624 cal., 26g fat (6g sat. fat), 173mg chol., 754mg sod., 41g carb. (1g sugars, 1g fiber), 53g pro.

Taco Noodle Dish

While we were housebound during a snowstorm, I got creative and used ingredients I had on hand to come up with this hearty casserole. Later, I modified it so now it has less fat and fewer calories.
—JUDY MUNGER WARREN, MN

START TO FINISH: 30 MIN.
MAKES: 6 SERVINGS

- **3 cups uncooked wide egg noodles**
- **2 pounds lean ground turkey**
- **1 envelope reduced-sodium taco seasoning**
- **1 teaspoon onion powder**
- **1 teaspoon chili powder**
- **½ teaspoon garlic powder**
- **1 can (8 ounces) tomato sauce**
- **1 can (4 ounces) chopped green chilies**
- **½ cup water**
- **1 cup shredded cheddar cheese**

TOPPINGS

- **2 cups shredded lettuce**
- **2 medium tomatoes, chopped**
- **⅓ cup sliced ripe olives**
- **½ cup taco sauce**
- **½ cup fat-free sour cream**

1. Preheat oven to 350°. Cook noodles according to package directions for al dente; drain.

2. Meanwhile, in a large nonstick skillet, cook and crumble turkey over medium-high heat until no longer pink, 6-8 minutes; drain. Stir in the seasonings, tomato sauce, chilies and water; bring to a boil. Reduce heat; simmer, uncovered, 5 minutes.

3. Spread noodles in a 11x7-in. baking dish coated with cooking spray. Top with turkey mixture; sprinkle with cheese. Bake, uncovered, until the cheese is melted, 10-15 minutes.

4. Top casserole with lettuce, tomatoes, olives and taco sauce. Serve with the sour cream.

NUTRITION FACTS 1 serving: 455 cal., 20g fat (7g sat. fat), 140mg chol., 954mg sod., 27g carb. (7g sugars, 3g fiber), 40g pro.

Spicy Peanut Chicken & Noodles

This simple recipe tastes like it took hours to make. It has the perfect levels of heat and spice for our family.
—**SHARON COLLISON** NEWARK, DE

START TO FINISH: 30 MIN.
MAKES: 4 SERVINGS

- 1 package (10.8 ounces) frozen broccoli, carrot and sugar snap pea blend
- 3/4 cup reduced-sodium chicken broth
- 1/3 cup creamy peanut butter
- 1/4 cup teriyaki sauce
- 1/4 teaspoon pepper
- 1/4 teaspoon cayenne pepper
- 1 cup coarsely shredded rotisserie chicken
- 1 package (8.8 ounces) thick rice noodles
- 3 green onions, thinly sliced on a diagonal
- Additional chicken broth, optional

1. Microwave frozen vegetables according to the package directions.

2. Place broth, peanut butter, teriyaki sauce, pepper and cayenne in a large skillet; cook and stir over medium heat until blended. Stir in chicken; heat through. Stir in vegetables.

3. Prepare noodles according to package directions. Drain and immediately add to chicken mixture, tossing to combine. Sprinkle with green onions. If desired, moisten with additional broth. Serve immediately.

NUTRITION FACTS 1 serving: 489 cal., 14g fat (3g sat. fat), 31mg chol., 971mg sod., 68g carb. (8g sugars, 4g fiber), 22g pro.

Skillet Ham & Rice

Ham, rice and mushrooms make a tasty combination in this homey stovetop dish. It's both fast and satisfying.

—SUSAN ZIVEC REGINA, SK

START TO FINISH: 25 MIN.
MAKES: 2 SERVINGS

- 1 teaspoon olive oil
- 1 medium onion, chopped
- 1 cup sliced fresh mushrooms
- 1 cup cubed fully cooked ham
- 1/8 teaspoon pepper
- 1/2 cup reduced-sodium chicken broth
- 1/4 cup water
- 3/4 cup uncooked instant rice
- 2 green onions, sliced
- 1/4 cup shredded Parmesan cheese

1. In a large nonstick skillet, heat oil over medium-high heat; saute onion and mushrooms until tender. Stir in ham, pepper, broth and water; bring to a boil. Stir in rice. Reduce heat; simmer, covered, until rice is tender, about 5 minutes.

2. Fluff with a fork. Top with green onions and cheese.

NOTE Look for lower-sodium versions of ham in the meat and deli sections. They typically have 25%-30% less.

NUTRITION FACTS 1 1/4 cups: 322 cal., 8g fat (3g sat. fat), 49mg chol., 1168mg sod., 38g carb. (4g sugars, 2g fiber), 24g pro.

Spicy Cajun Sausage & Rice Skillet

I created this easy skillet dish to use up the boil-in-a-bag rice in my cabinet. The result packs a lot of flavor.

—**SONALI RUDER** NEW YORK, NY

START TO FINISH: 30 MIN.
MAKES: 4 SERVINGS

- 1 package (16 ounces) hot lean turkey breakfast sausage
- 1 large onion, chopped
- 1 medium green pepper, chopped
- 1 can (14½ ounces) diced tomatoes with garlic and onion, undrained
- 1 can (14½ ounces) reduced-sodium chicken broth
- 3 teaspoons Cajun seasoning
- ¼ teaspoon pepper
- 2 bags boil-in-bag white rice
- Louisiana-style hot sauce, optional

1. In a large nonstick skillet, cook and crumble sausage with onion and pepper over medium-high heat until no longer pink, 5-7 minutes.

2. Stir in the tomatoes, broth, Cajun seasoning, pepper and contents of the rice bags; bring to a boil. Reduce heat; simmer, covered, until liquid is absorbed and the rice is tender, 8-10 minutes. If desired, serve with hot sauce.

NOTE For a light version of this recipe, replace half the sausage with lean ground turkey. Using unsalted chicken broth will also save almost 700mg sodium.

NUTRITION FACTS 1½ cups: 461 cal., 12g fat (3g sat. fat), 122mg chol., 1816mg sod., 52g carb. (6g sugars, 4g fiber), 35g pro.

FREEZE IT (5) INGREDIENTS

Chicken Enchilada Bake

Your family is going to gobble up this cheesy, southwestern chicken bake...and will ask for it again and again. It's real comfort food!

—MELANIE BURNS PUEBLO WEST, CO

PREP: 20 MIN. • **BAKE:** 50 MIN. + STANDING
MAKES: 10 SERVINGS

4½ cups shredded rotisserie chicken
1 can (28 ounces) green enchilada sauce
1¼ cups (10 ounces) sour cream
9 corn tortillas (6 inches), cut into 1½-inch pieces
4 cups shredded Monterey Jack cheese

1. Preheat oven to 375°. In a greased 13x9-in. baking dish, layer half of each of the following: chicken, enchilada sauce, sour cream, tortillas and cheese. Repeat layers.

2. Bake, covered, 40 minutes. Uncover; bake until bubbly, about 10 minutes. Let stand 15 minutes before serving.

FREEZE OPTION Cover and freeze unbaked casserole. To use, partially thaw in refrigerator overnight. Remove from refrigerator 30 minutes before baking. Preheat oven to 375°. Bake casserole as directed, increasing time as necessary to heat through and for a thermometer inserted in center to read 165°.

NUTRITION FACTS 1 cup: 469 cal., 29g fat (14g sat. fat), 113mg chol., 1077mg sod., 16g carb. (3g sugars, 1g fiber), 34g pro.

Garlic Shrimp & Rice Salad

For this easy-to-make main-dish salad, you can prepare the rice mixture and chop the vegetables ahead of time. Cook the shrimp at the last minute, then assemble it all for a light and pleasing meal.

—**DIANE NEMITZ** LUDINGTON, MI

START TO FINISH: 30 MIN.
MAKES: 4 SERVINGS

- 1 pound uncooked shrimp (31-40 per pound), peeled and deveined
- 2 tablespoons olive oil
- 2 garlic cloves, minced
- 1 teaspoon dried oregano
- 1 package (8.8 ounces) ready-to-serve brown rice
- ¼ cup mayonnaise
- ¼ cup sour cream
- 2 tablespoons minced fresh basil or 1 teaspoon dried basil
- 2 tablespoons lemon juice
- 1 celery rib, chopped
- ¼ cup minced fresh parsley
- 2 tablespoons chopped green pepper
- 4 cups fresh baby arugula or baby spinach

1. Toss shrimp with oil, garlic and oregano; let stand 15 minutes. Meanwhile, cook rice according to package directions. Transfer rice to a large bowl; cool slightly. For the dressing, mix mayonnaise, sour cream, basil and lemon juice.

2. In a large skillet, saute shrimp mixture over medium-high heat until the shrimp turn pink, 2-3 minutes. Add to rice; stir in celery, parsley and pepper. Add arugula and toss lightly; serve salad with the dressing.

NUTRITION FACTS 1 serving: 397 cal., 23g fat (5g sat. fat), 142mg chol., 232mg sod., 21g carb. (1g sugars, 2g fiber), 22g pro.

DID YOU KNOW?

Arugula has a peppery taste and tender leaves. If you're looking for a substitute, try a mix of baby spinach and watercress to give you both the dark green color and the spicy taste. A general spring mix (which usually includes some arugula) also works well.

Tandoori Chicken Pita Pizzas

My family and I are big picnickers, and I'm always looking for new dishes to try in the great outdoors. The amazing flavors at our favorite Indian restaurant inspired these mini pizzas.

—**ANGELA SPENGLER** TAMPA, FL

START TO FINISH: 25 MIN.
MAKES: 4 SERVINGS

- 1 cup plain Greek yogurt, divided
- 2 tablespoons chopped fresh cilantro
- ½ teaspoon ground coriander
- ½ teaspoon ground cumin
- ½ teaspoon ground ginger
- ½ teaspoon ground turmeric
- ½ teaspoon paprika
- ½ teaspoon cayenne pepper
- ¾ pound boneless skinless chicken breasts, cut into ½-inch-thick strips
- 4 whole wheat pita breads (6 inches)
- ⅔ cup crumbled feta cheese
- ⅓ cup chopped seeded tomato
- ⅓ cup chopped fresh Italian parsley

1. For sauce, in a small bowl mix ½ cup yogurt and cilantro. In a large bowl, mix spices and remaining yogurt; stir in chicken to coat.

2. Place chicken on an oiled grill rack over medium heat; grill, covered, until no longer pink, 2-3 minutes per side. Grill pita breads until warmed, about 1 minute per side.

3. Spread pitas with sauce. Top with chicken, cheese, tomato and parsley.

NUTRITION FACTS 1 pizza: 380 cal., 12g fat (6g sat. fat), 72mg chol., 598mg sod., 41g carb. (5g sugars, 5g fiber), 29g pro. ***Diabetic Exchanges:*** 3 lean meat, 2½ starch.

Roasted Vegetables with Sage, p. 140

CHAPTER 5

SIDES, SALADS & MORE

Make a great meal even better with one of these fabulous side dishes!

Colcannon Irish Potatoes 132
Parmesan Roasted Broccoli 135
Three-Bean Baked Beans 136
Tarragon Asparagus Salad 139
Roasted Vegetables with Sage 140
Grilled Peach, Rice & Arugula Salad. . . 143
Fabulous Green Beans. 144
Cheesy Cheddar Broccoli Casserole. . . 147
Almond Strawberry Salad. 148
Creamy Lemon Rice. 151
Spring Asparagus. 152
Bacon Avocado Salad 155
Olive & Onion Quick Bread. 156
Lemon Garlic Mushrooms. 159
Yummy Corn Chip Salad 160

5 INGREDIENTS

Colcannon Irish Potatoes

My mother came from Ireland as a teen and brought this homey recipe with her. It's great way to get my family to eat cooked cabbage—hidden in Grandma's potatoes!
—**MARIE PAGEL** LENA, WI

START TO FINISH: 30 MIN.
MAKES: 10 SERVINGS

- 2½ pounds potatoes (about 6 medium), peeled and cut into 1-inch pieces
- 2 cups chopped cabbage
- 1 large onion, chopped
- 1 teaspoon salt
- ¼ teaspoon pepper
- ¼ cup butter, softened
- 1 cup 2% milk

1. Place potatoes in a 6-qt. stockpot; add water to cover. Bring to a boil. Reduce heat to medium; cook, covered, until potatoes are almost tender, 8-10 minutes.

2. Add cabbage and onion; cook, covered, until cabbage is tender, 5-7 minutes. Drain; return to the pot. Add salt and pepper; mash to desired consistency, gradually adding butter and milk.

NUTRITION FACTS ¾ cup: 129 cal., 5g fat (3g sat. fat), 14mg chol., 290mg sod., 19g carb. (4g sugars, 2g fiber), 3g pro. ***Diabetic Exchanges:*** 1 starch, 1 fat.

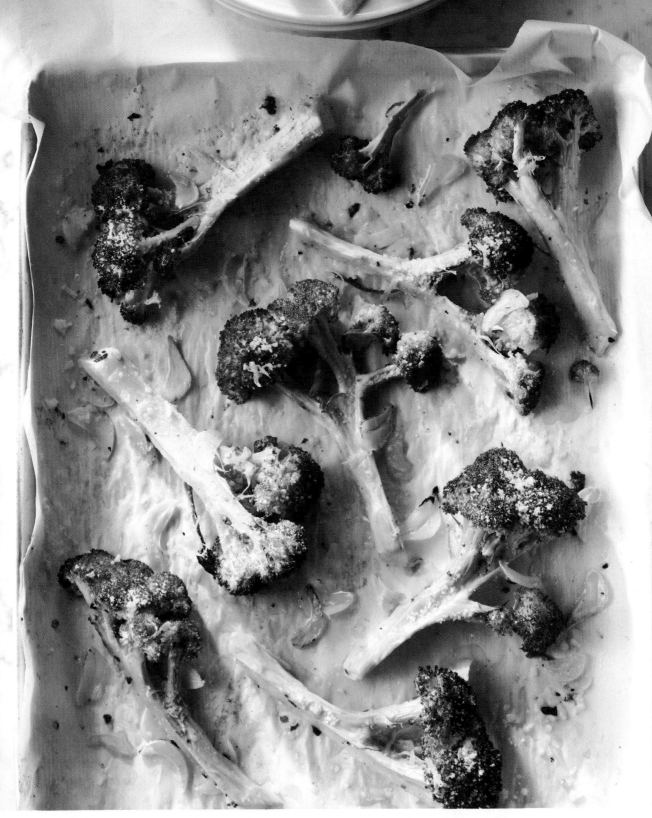

⑤ INGREDIENTS

Parmesan Roasted Broccoli

Sure, it's simple and healthy but, oh, is this roasted broccoli delicious! Cutting the stalks into tall trees turns this ordinary veggie into a standout side dish.

—**HOLLY SANDER** WELLESLEY, MA

START TO FINISH: 30 MIN.
MAKES: 4 SERVINGS

- 2 small broccoli crowns (about 8 ounces each)
- 3 tablespoons olive oil
- ½ teaspoon salt
- ½ teaspoon pepper
- ¼ teaspoon crushed red pepper flakes
- 4 garlic cloves, thinly sliced
- 2 tablespoons grated Parmesan cheese
- 1 teaspoon grated lemon peel

1. Preheat oven to 425°. Cut the broccoli crowns into quarters from top to bottom. Drizzle with oil; sprinkle with seasonings. Place in a parchment paper-lined 15x10x1-in. pan.

2. Roast until crisp-tender, 10-12 minutes. Sprinkle with garlic; roast 5 minutes longer. Sprinkle with cheese; roast until cheese is melted and stalks of broccoli are tender, 2-4 minutes more. Sprinkle with lemon peel.

NUTRITION FACTS 2 broccoli pieces: 144 cal., 11g fat (2g sat. fat), 2mg chol., 378mg sod., 9g carb. (2g sugars, 3g fiber), 4g pro. ***Diabetic Exchanges:*** 2 fat, 1 vegetable.

FREEZE IT

Three-Bean Baked Beans

I got this recipe from an aunt and made a couple of changes to suit our tastes. With ground beef and bacon mixed in, these satisfying beans are a big hit at backyard barbecues and church picnics.

—JULIE CURRINGTON GAHANNA, OH

PREP: 15 MIN. • **BAKE:** 1 HOUR
MAKES: 12 SERVINGS

- ½ pound ground beef
- 5 bacon strips, diced
- ½ cup chopped onion
- ⅓ cup packed brown sugar
- ¼ cup sugar
- ¼ cup ketchup
- ¼ cup barbecue sauce
- 2 tablespoons molasses
- 2 tablespoons prepared mustard
- ½ teaspoon chili powder
- ½ teaspoon salt
- 2 cans (16 ounces each) pork and beans, undrained
- 1 can (16 ounces) butter beans, rinsed and drained
- 1 can (16 ounces) kidney beans, rinsed and drained

1. Preheat oven to 350°. In a large skillet, cook and crumble beef with bacon and onion over medium heat until beef is no longer pink; drain.

2. Stir in sugars, ketchup, barbecue sauce, molasses, mustard, chili powder and salt until blended. Stir in beans. Transfer to a greased 2½-qt. baking dish. Bake, covered, until beans reach desired thickness, about 1 hour.

FREEZE OPTION Freeze cooled bean mixture in freezer containers. To use, partially thaw in refrigerator overnight. Heat through in a saucepan, stirring occasionally and adding a little water if necessary.

NUTRITION FACTS ¾ cup: 269 cal., 8g fat (2g sat. fat), 19mg chol., 708mg sod., 42g carb. (21g sugars, 7g fiber), 13g pro.

(5) INGREDIENTS

Tarragon Asparagus Salad

I love asparagus. I love it even more when it's drizzled with my light, lemony vinaigrette dressing with a touch of tarragon. It's perfect as a side for fresh spring meals.

—LINDA LACEK WINTER PARK, FL

PREP: 15 MIN. + CHILLING • **COOK:** 5 MIN.
MAKES: 4 SERVINGS

- **2 tablespoons lemon juice**
- **2 tablespoons olive oil**
- **1 teaspoon minced fresh tarragon or 1/4 teaspoon dried tarragon**
- **1 garlic clove, minced**
- **1/2 teaspoon Dijon mustard**
- **1/4 teaspoon pepper**
- **Dash salt**
- **1 pound fresh asparagus, cut into 2-inch pieces**

1. Place first seven ingredients in a jar with a tight-fitting lid; shake well. Refrigerate at least 1 hour.

2. In a large skillet, bring 1/2 in. of water to a boil. Add asparagus; cook, covered, until crisp-tender, 1-3 minutes. Remove asparagus and immediately drop into ice water. Drain and pat dry. Refrigerate, covered, until serving.

3. To serve, shake dressing again. Spoon over asparagus.

NUTRITION FACTS 1 serving: 77 cal., 7g fat (1g sat. fat), 0 chol., 387mg sod., 3g carb. (1g sugars, 1g fiber), 2g pro. ***Diabetic Exchanges:*** 1 1/2 fat, 1 vegetable.

Roasted Vegetables with Sage

When I can't decide what veggie to serve, I just roast a bunch. That's how we boost the veggie love at our house.

—**BETTY FULKS** ONIA, AR

PREP: 20 MIN. • **BAKE:** 35 MIN.
MAKES: 8 SERVINGS

- **5 cups cubed peeled butternut squash**
- **½ pound fingerling potatoes (about 2 cups)**
- **1 cup fresh Brussels sprouts, halved**
- **1 cup fresh baby carrots**
- **3 tablespoons butter**
- **1 tablespoon minced fresh sage or 1 teaspoon dried sage leaves**
- **1 garlic clove, minced**
- **½ teaspoon salt**

1. Preheat oven to 425°. Place vegetables in a large bowl. In a microwave, melt butter; stir in remaining ingredients. Add to vegetables and toss to coat.

2. Transfer to a greased 15x10x1-in. baking pan. Roast 35-45 minutes or until tender, stirring occasionally.

NUTRITION FACTS ¾ cup: 122 cal., 5g fat (3g sat. fat), 11mg chol., 206mg sod., 20g carb. (4g sugars, 3g fiber), 2g pro. ***Diabetic Exchanges:*** 1 starch, 1 fat.

Grilled Peach, Rice & Arugula Salad

I created this hearty salad when I needed to clear out some leftovers from the fridge—and it became an instant hit! The grilled peaches are the ultimate tastes-like-summer salad booster.

—LAUREN WYLER DRIPPING SPRINGS, TX

START TO FINISH: 30 MIN.
MAKES: 6 SERVINGS

- 3 tablespoons cider vinegar
- 2 tablespoons Dijon mustard
- 2 tablespoons canola oil
- 2 tablespoons maple syrup
- 1 tablespoon finely chopped shallot
- ¼ teaspoon cayenne pepper

SALAD

- 1 package (8.8 ounces) ready-to-serve long grain and wild rice
- 2 medium peaches, quartered
- 6 cups fresh arugula (about 4 ounces)
- 6 bacon strips, cooked and crumbled
- ½ cup crumbled goat cheese

1. For dressing, whisk together the first six ingredients.

2. Prepare rice according to package directions; cool slightly. Place peaches on an oiled grill rack over medium heat. Grill, covered, until lightly browned, 6-8 minutes, turning occasionally.

3. To serve, add bacon and ¼ cup dressing to rice. Line a platter with arugula; top with rice mixture and peaches. Drizzle with remaining dressing; top with cheese.

NUTRITION FACTS 1 serving: 218 cal., 11g fat (3g sat. fat), 20mg chol., 530mg sod., 23g carb. (9g sugars, 2g fiber), 7g pro. ***Diabetic Exchanges:*** 1 starch, 1 vegetable, 2 fat.

5 INGREDIENTS

Fabulous Green Beans

My family loves this butter sauce over green beans whether they are fresh or frozen. I've used this easy sauce over sugar snap peas as well.

—**LORI DANIELS** BEVERLY, WV

START TO FINISH: 20 MIN.
MAKES: 4 SERVINGS

- **1 pound fresh green beans, trimmed**
- **¼ cup butter, cubed**
- **1 tablespoon olive oil**
- **½ teaspoon salt**
- **½ teaspoon Italian seasoning**
- **½ teaspoon lemon juice**
- **¼ teaspoon grated lemon peel**

1. Place beans in a steamer basket; place in a large saucepan over 1 in. of water. Bring to a boil; cover and steam for 8-10 minutes or until crisp-tender.

2. Meanwhile, in a small saucepan, heat the remaining ingredients until butter is melted. Transfer beans to a serving bowl; drizzle with butter mixture and toss to coat.

HERBED-BUTTER GREEN BEANS Saute ¼ cup chopped onion, ¼ cup chopped celery, 2 tablespoons sesame seeds, 3 minced garlic cloves, 4 teaspoons dried parsley flakes, ½ teaspoon salt, ½ teaspoon dried basil, ½ teaspoon dried oregano and ⅛ teaspoon crushed dried rosemary in 3 tablespoons butter until the vegetables are tender. Toss with steamed beans.

SPICED GREEN BEANS Toss steamed beans with 2 tablespoons melted butter, ¼ teaspoon celery seed, ¼ teaspoon ground ginger, ¼ teaspoon ground mustard and ¼ teaspoon salt.

DILLED GREEN BEANS Toss steamed beans with 2 tablespoons rice vinegar, 2 tablespoons soy sauce, 1 tablespoon snipped fresh dill and 1 tablespoon toasted sesame seeds.

NUTRITION FACTS ¾ cup: 165 cal., 15g fat (8g sat. fat), 30mg chol., 382mg sod., 8g carb. (2g sugars, 4g fiber), 2g pro.

5 INGREDIENTS

Cheesy Cheddar Broccoli Casserole

People who don't even like broccoli beg me to make this comforting recipe. It's similar to a classic green bean casserole, but the melted cheese just puts it over the top.
—**ELAINE HUBBARD** POCONO LAKE, PA

PREP: 15 MIN. • **BAKE:** 35 MIN.
MAKES: 8 SERVINGS

- **1 can (10¾ ounces) condensed cream of mushroom soup, undiluted**
- **1 cup (8 ounces) sour cream**
- **1½ cups shredded sharp cheddar cheese, divided**
- **1 can (6 ounces) french-fried onions, divided**
- **2 packages (16 ounces each) frozen broccoli florets, thawed**

1. Preheat oven to 325°. In a large saucepan, combine soup, sour cream, 1 cup cheese and 1¼ cups onions; heat through over medium heat, stirring until blended, 4-5 minutes. Stir in broccoli. Transfer to a greased 2-qt. baking dish.

2. Bake, uncovered, until bubbly, 25-30 minutes. Sprinkle with the remaining cheese and onions. Bake until cheese is melted, 10-15 minutes.

NUTRITION FACTS ¾ cup: 359 cal., 26g fat (11g sat. fat), 30mg chol., 641mg sod., 19g carb. (4g sugars, 3g fiber), 8g pro.

Almond Strawberry Salad

It's easy to love this pretty salad topped with strawberries and sliced almonds. While it has just a few ingredients, it's loaded with flavor.

—RENAE ROSSOW UNION, KY

START TO FINISH: 10 MIN.
MAKES: 4 SERVINGS

- **3 cups fresh baby spinach**
- **½ cup sliced fresh strawberries**
- **¼ cup honey-roasted sliced almonds**
- **1 tablespoon cider vinegar**
- **1 tablespoon honey**
- **1½ teaspoons sugar**

Place spinach, strawberries and almonds in a large bowl. Mix vinegar, honey and sugar until blended; toss with the salad.

NUTRITION FACTS ¾ cup: 75 cal., 4g fat (0 sat. fat), 0 chol., 98mg sod., 9g carb. (8g sugars, 1g fiber), 2g pro. ***Diabetic Exchanges:*** 1 vegetable, 1 fat.

Creamy Lemon Rice

This bright rice dish has a creamy texture that's reminiscent of a lemon risotto, but without all the careful adding and stirring. Keep this one in your back pocket for hosting dinner guests—or as a great side for any old day!

—**LYNDSAY WELLS** LADYSMITH, BC

START TO FINISH: 30 MIN.
MAKES: 4 SERVINGS

2½ cups chicken broth
2 ounces cream cheese, cubed
½ teaspoon grated lemon peel
1 tablespoon lemon juice
¼ teaspoon salt
¼ teaspoon coarsely ground pepper
1 cup uncooked long grain rice
¼ cup minced fresh basil

1. In a saucepan, combine first six ingredients; bring to a boil. Stir with a whisk to blend.

2. Stir in the rice; return to a boil. Reduce heat; simmer, covered, until liquid is absorbed and rice is tender, about 15 minutes. Stir in basil.

NUTRITION FACTS ¾ cup: 246 cal., 6g fat (3g sat. fat), 17mg chol., 806mg sod., 42g carb. (1g sugars, 1g fiber), 5g pro.

Spring Asparagus

This fresh and colorful side dish is delicious whether served warm or cold. I get lots of compliments on the homemade dressing.
—MILLIE VICKERY LENA, IL

START TO FINISH: 25 MIN.
MAKES: 8 SERVINGS

- **1½ pounds fresh asparagus, trimmed and cut into 2-inch pieces**
- **2 small tomatoes, cut into wedges**
- **3 tablespoons cider vinegar**
- **¾ teaspoon Worcestershire sauce**
- **⅓ cup sugar**
- **1 tablespoon grated onion**
- **½ teaspoon salt**
- **½ teaspoon paprika**
- **⅓ cup canola oil**
- **⅓ cup sliced almonds, toasted**
- **⅓ cup crumbled blue cheese, optional**

1. In a large saucepan, bring 1 cup water to a boil. Add asparagus; cook, covered, until crisp-tender, 3-5 minutes. Drain; place in a large bowl. Add tomatoes; cover and keep warm.

2. Place vinegar, Worcestershire sauce, sugar, onion, salt and paprika in a blender; cover and process until smooth. While processing, gradually add oil in a steady stream. Toss with asparagus mixture. Top with almonds and, if desired, cheese.

NOTE To toast nuts, bake in a shallow pan in a 350° oven for 5-10 minutes or cook in a skillet over low heat until lightly browned, stirring occasionally.

NUTRITION FACTS ¾ cup: 154 cal., 11g fat (1g sat. fat), 0 chol., 159mg sod., 12g carb. (10g sugars, 1g fiber), 2g pro. *Diabetic Exchanges:* 2 fat, 1 vegetable, ½ starch.

Bacon Avocado Salad

Everyone in my family loves this summery salad—even the younger kids! I serve it at pretty much every get-together I've hosted, and at this point, the recipe's been shared too many times to count.

—NOREEN MCCORMICK DANEK CROMWELL, CT

START TO FINISH: 25 MIN.
MAKES: 10 SERVINGS

- **¾ cup extra virgin olive oil**
- **¼ cup red wine vinegar**
- **4 teaspoons sugar**
- **2 garlic cloves, minced**
- **1 teaspoon salt**
- **1 teaspoon Dijon mustard**

SALAD

- **1 bunch romaine, chopped (about 12 cups)**
- **¾ pound bacon strips, cooked and crumbled**
- **3 medium tomatoes, chopped**
- **1 medium red onion, halved and thinly sliced**
- **3 medium ripe avocados, peeled and cubed**
- **2 tablespoons lemon juice**
- **1 cup (4 ounces) crumbled Gorgonzola or feta cheese**

1. Place the first six ingredients in a jar with a tight-fitting lid; shake well until blended. Refrigerate until serving.

2. In a large bowl, combine romaine, bacon, tomatoes and onion. Toss avocados with lemon juice and add to the salad. Sprinkle with cheese. Serve with dressing, shaking to blend again if needed.

NUTRITION FACTS 1⅓ cups: 339 cal., 31g fat (7g sat. fat), 22mg chol., 626mg sod., 10g carb. (4g sugars, 5g fiber), 9g pro.

TOP TIP

Confused by the many different kinds of olive oil? Virgin or extra virgin olive oil smoke at low temperatures and have a more delicate flavor, making them perfect for cold foods and salad dressings. Save common olive oil for cooking at high heat.

Olive & Onion Quick Bread

I've been baking for over 50 years and never get tired of trying new recipes for my family, friends and co-workers. I feel like an artist creating a masterpiece of love. This savory loaf makes a great gift.

—**PAULA MARCHESI** LENHARTSVILLE, PA

PREP: 15 MIN. • **BAKE:** 45 MIN. + COOLING
MAKES: 1 LOAF (12 SLICES)

- 1 tablespoon canola oil
- 1 medium onion, finely chopped
- 2 cups all-purpose flour
- 1 tablespoon minced fresh rosemary
- 1 teaspoon baking soda
- ½ teaspoon salt
- 2 large eggs
- 1 cup buttermilk
- 2 tablespoons butter, melted
- ¼ cup plus 2 tablespoons sharp cheddar cheese, divided
- ¼ cup each chopped pitted green and ripe olives

1. Preheat oven to 350°. In a skillet, heat oil over medium-high heat. Add onion; cook and stir until tender, 2-3 minutes. Remove from heat.

2. In a large bowl, whisk flour, rosemary, baking soda and salt. In another bowl, whisk eggs, buttermilk and melted butter until blended. Add to the flour mixture; stir just until moistened. Fold in ¼ cup cheese, olives and onion.

3. Transfer to a greased 8x4-in. loaf pan. Bake 40 minutes. Sprinkle remaining cheese over top. Bake until a toothpick inserted in center comes out clean, 5-10 minutes longer. Cool in pan 10 minutes before removing to a wire rack to cool.

NUTRITION FACTS 1 slice: 150 cal., 6g fat (2g sat. fat), 41mg chol., 373mg sod., 18g carb. (1g sugars, 1g fiber), 5g pro.

(5) INGREDIENTS

Lemon Garlic Mushrooms

I baste whole mushrooms with a lemony sauce to prepare this simple side dish. Using skewers or a basket makes it easy to turn them as they grill to perfection.

—DIANE HIXON NICEVILLE, FL

START TO FINISH: 15 MIN.
MAKES: 4 SERVINGS

- **1/4 cup lemon juice**
- **3 tablespoons minced fresh parsley**
- **2 tablespoons olive oil**
- **3 garlic cloves, minced**
- **Pepper to taste**
- **1 pound large fresh mushrooms**

1. For dressing, whisk together first five ingredients. Toss mushrooms with 2 tablespoons of the dressing.

2. Grill mushrooms, covered, over medium-high heat until tender, 5-7 minutes per side. Toss with remaining dressing before serving.

NUTRITION FACTS 1 serving: 94 cal., 7g fat (1g sat. fat), 0mg chol., 2mg sod., 6g carb. (0g sugars, 0g fiber), 3g pro. *Diabetic Exchanges:* 1 vegetable, 1 1/2 fat.

Yummy Corn Chip Salad

Corn chips give an extra-special crunch and unexpected flavor to this potluck-favorite salad. Bacon adds a hint of smokiness while the cranberries bring a touch of sweetness. It's the perfect picnic companion!
—NORA FRIESEN ABERDEEN, MS

START TO FINISH: 25 MIN.
MAKES: 12 SERVINGS

- 3/4 cup canola oil
- 1/4 cup cider vinegar
- 1/4 cup mayonnaise
- 2 tablespoons yellow mustard
- 1/2 teaspoon salt
- 3/4 cup sugar
- 1/2 small onion
- 3/4 teaspoon poppy seeds

SALAD

- 2 bunches leaf lettuce, chopped (about 20 cups)
- 1 package (9 1/4 ounces) corn chips
- 8 bacon strips, cooked and crumbled
- 1 cup shredded part-skim mozzarella cheese
- 1 cup dried cranberries

1. For dressing, place the first seven ingredients in a blender. Cover; process until smooth. Stir in poppy seeds.

2. Place salad ingredients in a large bowl; toss with dressing. Serve immediately.

NUTRITION FACTS 1 1/3 cups: 436 cal., 30g fat (4g sat. fat), 12mg chol., 456mg sod., 38g carb. (24g sugars, 2g fiber), 7g pro.

TOP TIP

Instead of frying bacon, lay strips on a jelly-roll pan and bake at 350° for about 30 minutes. Prepared this way, bacon comes out crisp and flat. Plus, the pan cleans easily, and there's no stovetop spattering.
—Lou H., Mobridge, SD

Cheesy Broccoli Soup
in a Bread Bowl, p. 168

CHAPTER 6

SOUPS & SANDWICHES

Serve them on their own or pair them up for the perfect lunch or quick dinner.

Blue Cheese Chicken Salad Sandwiches 164
Indian Spiced Chickpea Wraps 167
Cheesy Broccoli Soup in a Bread Bowl 168
Jalapeno Burgers with Gorgonzola . . . 171
Shrimp Gazpacho 172
Curried Egg Salad 175
Italian Wedding Soup 176
Cold-Day Chicken Noodle Soup 179
Cashew Turkey Salad Sandwiches . . . 180
Lemony Chicken Soup 183
Mushroom Bacon Turkey Burgers . . . 184
Curried Chicken Corn Chowder 187
Mushroom & Onion Grilled Cheese Sandwiches 188
Quick Cream of Mushroom Soup 191

Blue Cheese Chicken Salad Sandwiches

I'm a big fan of blue cheese dressing, so I tried it in chicken salad instead of mayo. So tangy! Serve the chicken mixture on a bed of lettuce if you're in the mood for salad instead.
—**GIOVANNA KRANENBERG** CAMBRIDGE, MN

START TO FINISH: 15 MIN.
MAKES: 6 SERVINGS

- 2⁄3 cup chunky blue cheese salad dressing
- 1 celery rib, diced
- 1⁄2 cup seeded and diced cucumber
- 1⁄3 cup diced carrot
- 2 tablespoons finely chopped onion
- 1 garlic clove, minced
- 1⁄4 teaspoon salt
- 1⁄4 teaspoon pepper
- 2 cups shredded rotisserie chicken, chilled
- 12 slices sourdough bread
- Crumbled blue cheese, optional

Mix the first eight ingredients; stir in chicken. Spread over half of the bread slices. If desired, sprinkle with blue cheese. Top with remaining bread.

NUTRITION FACTS 1 sandwich: 418 cal., 19g fat (4g sat. fat), 50mg chol., 747mg sod., 40g carb. (5g sugars, 2g fiber), 22g pro.

Indian Spiced Chickpea Wraps

Raita, an Indian condiment made with yogurt, elevates this vegetarian dish to a satisfying gourmet wrap. If you're in the mood to experiment, substitute mango or cucumber for the pineapple and add fresh herbs like cilantro or mint.

—**JENNIFER BECKMAN** FALLS CHURCH, VA

START TO FINISH: 30 MIN.
MAKES: 4 SERVINGS

RAITA

- 1 cup (8 ounces) reduced-fat plain yogurt
- ½ cup unsweetened pineapple tidbits
- ¼ teaspoon salt
- ¼ teaspoon ground cumin

WRAPS

- 2 teaspoons canola oil
- 1 small onion, chopped
- 1 tablespoon minced fresh gingerroot
- 2 garlic cloves, minced
- ½ teaspoon curry powder
- ¼ teaspoon salt
- ¼ teaspoon ground coriander
- ¼ teaspoon ground cumin
- ¼ teaspoon cayenne pepper, optional
- 1 can (15 ounces) chickpeas or garbanzo beans, rinsed and drained
- 1 cup canned crushed tomatoes
- 3 cups fresh baby spinach
- 4 whole wheat tortillas (8 inches), warmed

1. For the pineapple raita, mix the first four ingredients.

2. For the wraps, in a large nonstick skillet coated with cooking spray, heat oil over medium-high heat; saute onion until tender. Add ginger, garlic and seasonings; cook and stir until fragrant, about 1 minute. Stir in chickpeas and tomatoes; bring to a boil. Reduce heat; simmer, uncovered, until slightly thickened, 5-8 minutes, stirring the mixture occasionally.

3. To serve, place spinach and chickpea mixture on tortillas. Top with raita and roll up.

NUTRITION FACTS 1 wrap: 321 cal., 7g fat (1g sat. fat), 3mg chol., 734mg sod., 55g carb. (15g sugars, 10g fiber), 13g pro.

Cheesy Broccoli Soup in a Bread Bowl

This creamy, cheesy broccoli soup tastes just like the soup you get at Panera Bread. My family requests it all the time. You can even make your own bread bowls!

—RACHEL PREUS MARSHALL, MI

PREP: 5 MIN. • **COOK:** 30 MIN.
MAKES: 6 SERVINGS

- **¼ cup butter, cubed**
- **½ cup chopped onion**
- **2 garlic cloves, minced**
- **4 cups fresh broccoli florets (about 8 ounces)**
- **1 large carrot, finely chopped**
- **3 cups chicken stock**
- **2 cups half-and-half cream**
- **2 bay leaves**
- **½ teaspoon salt**
- **¼ teaspoon ground nutmeg**
- **¼ teaspoon pepper**
- **¼ cup cornstarch**
- **¼ cup water or additional chicken stock**
- **2½ cups shredded cheddar cheese**
- **6 small round bread loaves (about 8 ounces each)**

1. In a 6-qt. stockpot, heat butter over medium heat; saute the onion and garlic until tender, 6-8 minutes. Stir in broccoli, carrot, stock, cream and seasonings; bring to a boil. Simmer, uncovered, until the vegetables are tender, 10-12 minutes.

2. Mix cornstarch and water until smooth; stir into soup. Bring to a boil, stirring occasionally; cook and stir until thickened, 1-2 minutes. Remove bay leaves. Stir in cheese until melted.

3. Cut a slice off the top of each bread loaf; hollow out the bottoms, leaving ¼-in.-thick shells (save removed bread for another use). Fill with soup just before serving.

NUTRITION FACTS 1 cup (calculated without bread bowl): 422 cal., 32g fat (19g sat. fat), 107mg chol., 904mg sod., 15g carb. (5g sugars, 2g fiber), 17g pro.

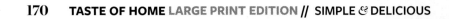

Jalapeno Burgers with Gorgonzola

On a whim, we mixed homemade jalapeno jam into ground beef patties, then topped the burgers with caramelized onions and tangy Gorgonzola cheese. Fabulous!

—BECKY MOLLENKAMP ST. LOUIS, MO

START TO FINISH: 30 MIN.
MAKES: 4 SERVINGS

- 1 tablespoon canola oil
- 1 teaspoon butter
- 1 medium onion, halved and thinly sliced
- Dash salt
- Dash sugar

BURGERS

- 1/3 cup jalapeno pepper jelly
- 1/2 teaspoon salt
- 1/4 teaspoon pepper
- 1 pound ground beef
- 4 hamburger buns, split and toasted
- 2 tablespoons crumbled Gorgonzola cheese
- Thinly sliced jalapeno pepper, optional

1. In a small skillet, heat oil and butter over medium heat. Add onion, salt and sugar; cook and stir 3-4 minutes or until onion is softened. Reduce heat to medium-low; cook 4-6 minutes or until deep golden brown, stirring occasionally.

2. In a large bowl, mix jelly, salt and pepper. Add the ground beef; mix lightly but thoroughly. Shape into four 1/2-in.-thick patties.

3. Grill burgers, covered, over medium heat or broil 4 in. from heat 4-5 minutes on each side or until a thermometer reads 160°. Serve on buns and top with caramelized onion, cheese and, if desired, sliced jalapeno.

NUTRITION FACTS 1 burger: 460 cal., 20g fat (7g sat. fat), 76mg chol., 669mg sod., 43g carb. (18g sugars, 2g fiber), 25g pro.

Shrimp Gazpacho

Here's a refreshing take on the classic chilled tomato soup. Our twist features shrimp, lime and plenty of avocado.
—*TASTE OF HOME* TEST KITCHEN

PREP: 15 MIN. + CHILLING
MAKES: 12 SERVINGS (ABOUT 3 QUARTS)

- **6 cups spicy hot V8 juice**
- **2 cups cold water**
- **½ cup lime juice**
- **½ cup minced fresh cilantro**
- **½ teaspoon salt**
- **¼ to ½ teaspoon hot pepper sauce**
- **1 pound peeled and deveined cooked shrimp (31-40 per pound), tails removed**
- **1 medium cucumber, seeded and diced**
- **2 medium tomatoes, seeded and chopped**
- **2 medium ripe avocados, peeled and chopped**

In a large nonreactive bowl, mix first six ingredients, Gently stir in remaining ingredients. Refrigerate, covered, for 1 hour before serving.

NOTE This recipe is best served the same day it's made.

NUTRITION FACTS 1 cup: 112 cal., 4g fat (1g sat. fat), 57mg chol., 399mg sod., 9g carb. (5g sugars, 3g fiber), 10g pro. ***Diabetic Exchanges:*** 1 lean meat, 2 vegetable, 1 fat.

Curried Egg Salad

Made with curry and ginger, my take on egg salad is an exciting departure from the norm. We eat it often in the summer.

—JOYCE MCDOWELL WEST UNION, OH

START TO FINISH: 15 MIN.
MAKES: 6 SERVINGS

- ½ cup mayonnaise
- ½ teaspoon ground curry
- ½ teaspoon honey
- Dash ground ginger
- 6 hard-boiled large eggs, coarsely chopped
- 3 green onions, sliced
- 6 slices whole wheat bread
- Tomato slices and cracked pepper, optional

Mix the first four ingredients; stir in eggs and green onions. Spread on bread. If desired, top with tomato and sprinkle with pepper.

NOTE A simple switch to low-fat mayonnaise will save 100 cal. and more than 10g fat.

NUTRITION FACTS 1 open-faced sandwich: 273 cal., 20g fat (4g sat. fat), 188mg chol., 284mg sod., 14g carb. (2g sugars, 2g fiber), 10g pro.

Italian Wedding Soup

My husband and I had an amazing soup with orzo in a little Italian restaurant. I tweaked it at home to make it healthier but kept the warm, comforting flavor.

—BARBARA SPITZER LODI, CA

START TO FINISH: 30 MIN.
MAKES: 6 SERVINGS

- **1 package (19½ ounces) Italian turkey sausage links, casings removed**
- **2 shallots, finely chopped**
- **3 garlic cloves, minced**
- **1 carton (32 ounces) reduced-sodium chicken broth**
- **¾ cup uncooked whole wheat orzo pasta**
- **¼ teaspoon pepper**
- **10 cups coarsely chopped escarole or spinach**
- **½ cup coarsely chopped fresh Italian parsley**

1. In a 6-qt. stockpot, cook sausage, shallots and garlic over medium heat 6-8 minutes or until the sausage is no longer pink, breaking up sausage into crumbles. Drain.

2. Add broth to sausage mixture; bring to a boil. Stir in orzo, pepper and escarole; return to a boil. Reduce heat; simmer, uncovered, 10-12 minutes or until orzo is tender. Stir in parsley before serving.

NUTRITION FACTS 1 cup: 197 cal., 6g fat (1g sat. fat), 34mg chol., 780mg sod., 20g carb. (1g sugars, 6g fiber), 16g pro.

HOW TO

CHIFFONADE SPINACH

For a pretty presentation, make long, even strips of leafy vegetables like spinach and escarole. Stack the leaves neatly in the same direction, then roll the stack lengthwise into a tight cigar shape. Slice across the rolled leaves to create thin strips.

Cold-Day Chicken Noodle Soup

When I was sick, my mom would stir up a heartwarming chicken noodle soup. It's so soothing for colds and cold-weather days.
—ANTHONY GRAHAM OTTAWA, IL

PREP: 15 MIN. • **COOK:** 25 MIN.
MAKES: 8 SERVINGS (3 QUARTS)

- 1 tablespoon canola oil
- 2 celery ribs, chopped
- 2 medium carrots, chopped
- 1 medium onion, chopped
- 8 cups reduced-sodium chicken broth
- ½ teaspoon dried basil
- ¼ teaspoon pepper
- 3 cups uncooked whole wheat egg noodles (about 4 ounces)
- 3 cups coarsely chopped rotisserie chicken
- 1 tablespoon minced fresh parsley

1. In a 6-qt. stockpot, heat the oil over medium-high heat. Add celery, carrots and onion; cook and stir 5-7 minutes or until tender.

2. Add broth, basil and pepper; bring to a boil. Stir in noodles; cook 12-14 minutes or until al dente. Stir in chicken and parsley; heat through.

NOTE Can chicken noodle soup really help ease cold symptoms? A number of scientific studies actually support the idea that it can.

NUTRITION FACTS 1½ cups: 195 cal., 6g fat (1g sat. fat), 47mg chol., 639mg sod., 16g carb. (2g sugars, 3g fiber), 21g pro. ***Diabetic Exchanges:*** 2 lean meat, 1 starch, ½ fat.

Cashew Turkey Salad Sandwiches

One of the best parts of the Thanksgiving season is turkey sandwiches! In our house, we use turkey, apricots and cashews tucked inside slices of pumpernickel for a top-notch sandwich.

—**MARY WILHELM** SPARTA, WI

START TO FINISH: 15 MIN.
MAKES: 4 SERVINGS

¼ cup reduced-fat mayonnaise
2 tablespoons reduced-fat plain yogurt
1 green onion, chopped
¼ teaspoon salt
¼ teaspoon pepper
1½ cups cubed cooked turkey breast
¼ cup thinly sliced celery
2 tablespoons chopped dried apricots
2 tablespoons chopped unsalted cashews
8 slices pumpernickel bread
4 lettuce leaves

1. In a bowl, mix the first five ingredients. Stir in turkey, celery, apricots and cashews.

2. Line half of the bread slices with lettuce. Top with turkey mixture and remaining bread.

NUTRITION FACTS 1 sandwich: 298 cal., 9g fat (2g sat. fat), 51mg chol., 664mg sod., 32g carb. (4g sugars, 4g fiber), 22g pro. ***Diabetic Exchanges:*** 2 starch, 2 lean meat, 1½ fat.

Lemony Chicken Soup

While living in California, I enjoyed a delicious chicken-lemon soup at a local restaurant. When I returned to Texas, I experimented with many versions before landing on this one.
—**BRENDA TOLLETT** SAN ANTONIO, TX

START TO FINISH: 25 MIN.
MAKES: 8 SERVINGS (2 QUARTS)

- 1/3 cup butter, cubed
- 3/4 cup all-purpose flour
- 6 cups chicken broth
- 1 cup whole milk
- 1 cup half-and-half cream
- 1 1/2 cups cubed cooked chicken
- 1 tablespoon lemon juice
- 1/2 teaspoon salt
- 1/8 teaspoon pepper
- Dash ground nutmeg
- Lemon wedges

1. In a large heavy saucepan, melt butter. Stir in flour until smooth; gradually whisk in broth, milk and cream. Bring to a boil; cook and stir until thickened, about 2 minutes.

2. Stir in chicken, lemon juice and seasonings; heat through over medium heat, stirring occasionally. Serve with lemon wedges.

NUTRITION FACTS 1 cup: 231 cal., 14g fat (8g sat. fat), 66mg chol., 994mg sod., 12g carb. (3g sugars, 0 fiber), 12g pro.

Mushroom Bacon Turkey Burgers

If you ask me, a good burger needs some mushrooms on top, but they tend to slide around and fall out. So I decided to chop the mushrooms and put them right into the patties—problem solved!
—MELISSA OBERNESSER UTICA, NY

START TO FINISH: 30 MIN.
MAKES: 4 SERVINGS

- 1 cup finely chopped fresh mushrooms (about 4 medium)
- 3 tablespoons soft bread crumbs
- 3 tablespoons barbecue sauce
- ¾ teaspoon onion powder
- ½ teaspoon garlic powder
- ¼ teaspoon pepper
- 1 pound extra-lean ground turkey
- 4 turkey bacon strips, halved
- 4 thin slices cheddar cheese
- 4 whole wheat hamburger buns, split
- Additional barbecue sauce
- Dill pickle slices, optional

1. Combine the first six ingredients. Add turkey; mix lightly but thoroughly. Shape into four ½-in.-thick patties.

2. Place burgers on an oiled grill rack over medium heat; grill, covered, until a thermometer reads 165°, 4-5 minutes per side. Grill bacon strips, covered, until crisp, 2-3 minutes per side. Top burgers with cheese and bacon; grill, covered, until cheese is melted, 30 seconds.

3. Serve on buns. Top with additional barbecue sauce and, if desired, pickles.

NOTE To make soft bread crumbs, tear bread into pieces and place in a food processor or blender. Cover and pulse until crumbs form. One slice of bread yields ½ to ¾ cup crumbs.

NUTRITION FACTS 1 burger: 389 cal., 17g fat (4g sat. fat), 95mg chol., 727mg sod., 30g carb. (9g sugars, 4g fiber), 32g pro. ***Diabetic Exchanges:*** 4 lean meat, 2 starch, 2 fat.

Curried Chicken Corn Chowder

Here's the ultimate breezy-day chowder. It's my version of a family recipe.
—KENDRA DOSS COLORADO SPRINGS, CO

PREP: 15 MIN. • **COOK:** 30 MIN.
MAKES: 8 SERVINGS (2 QUARTS)

- **1 tablespoon butter**
- **2 medium onions, chopped**
- **2 celery ribs, chopped**
- **2 teaspoons curry powder**
- **1/4 teaspoon salt**
- **1/4 teaspoon pepper**
- **Dash cayenne pepper**
- **5 cups frozen corn (about 25 ounces)**
- **3 cans (14 1/2 ounces each) reduced-sodium chicken broth**
- **1/2 cup all-purpose flour**
- **1/2 cup 2% milk**
- **3 cups cubed cooked chicken breast**
- **1/3 cup minced fresh cilantro**

1. In a Dutch oven, heat butter over medium heat. Add onions and celery; cook and stir until tender. Stir in seasonings; cook 30 seconds longer.

2. Stir in corn and broth; bring to a boil. Reduce heat and simmer, covered, for 15 minutes.

3. In a small bowl, whisk flour and milk until smooth; stir into soup. Bring to a boil; cook and stir 2 minutes or until thickened. Stir in chicken and cilantro; heat through.

NUTRITION FACTS 1 cup: 229 cal., 4g fat (2g sat. fat), 45mg chol., 582mg sod., 28g carb. (5g sugars, 3g fiber), 22g pro. *Diabetic Exchanges:* 2 starch, 2 lean meat.

Mushroom & Onion Grilled Cheese Sandwiches

Little ones might like plain grilled cheese, but why not kick things up a notch for everyone else at the table? We add bacon and baby portobello mushrooms to cheddar grilled cheese for this specialty. It's good to the last crumb.

—**BLAIR LONERGAN** ROCHELLE, VA

START TO FINISH: 25 MIN.
MAKES: 4 SERVINGS

- 3 tablespoons butter, softened, divided
- 8 ounces sliced baby portobello mushrooms
- 1 small onion, halved and thinly sliced
- 8 thin slices cheddar cheese (about 3 ounces)
- 8 slices Texas toast
- 4 bacon strips, cooked and crumbled

1. In a large nonstick skillet coated with cooking spray, heat 1 tablespoon butter over medium-high heat. Add mushrooms and onion; cook and stir 4-5 minutes or until tender. Remove from pan. Wipe skillet clean.

2. Place one slice of cheese on each of four bread slices. Top with mushroom mixture, bacon and the remaining cheese and bread. Lightly spread the outsides of the sandwiches with the remaining butter.

3. In same skillet, toast sandwiches in batches over medium heat 45-60 seconds on each side or until golden brown and cheese is melted.

NUTRITION FACTS 1 sandwich: 406 cal., 21g fat (11g sat. fat), 54mg chol., 729mg sod., 39g carb. (5g sugars, 2g fiber), 16g pro.

Quick Cream of Mushroom Soup

My daughter-in-law, a gourmet cook, served this soup as the first course for Thanksgiving dinner. She'd gotten the recipe from her mom and graciously shared it with me. Now I'm happy to share it with my own friends and family.

—**ANNE KULICK** PHILLIPSBURG, NJ

START TO FINISH: 30 MIN.
MAKES: 6 SERVINGS

- 2 tablespoons butter
- ½ pound sliced fresh mushrooms
- ¼ cup chopped onion
- 6 tablespoons all-purpose flour
- ½ teaspoon salt
- ⅛ teaspoon pepper
- 2 cans (14½ ounces each) chicken broth
- 1 cup half-and-half cream

1. In a large saucepan, heat butter over medium-high heat; saute mushrooms and onion until tender.

2. Mix flour, salt, pepper and one can broth until smooth; stir into mushroom mixture. Stir in remaining broth. Bring to a boil; cook and stir until thickened, about 2 minutes. Reduce heat; stir in cream. Simmer, uncovered, until flavors are blended, about 15 minutes, stirring occasionally.

NUTRITION FACTS 1 cup: 136 cal., 8g fat (5g sat. fat), 33mg chol., 842mg sod., 10g carb. (3g sugars, 1g fiber), 4g pro.

Chicken Fajita Chowder, p. 218

CHAPTER 7

SLOW-COOKED GREATS

From appetizers to desserts, a slow cooker has your meal ready when you want it.

Slow Cooker Sriracha Corn. 194
Slow Cooker Stuffed Pepper Soup 197
Thai Coconut Beef 198
Slow Cooker Cheddar
Bacon Ale Dip 201
Slow Cooker Bacon Mac & Cheese. . . .202
Simple Swedish Meatballs 205
Strawberry-Banana Pudding Cake. . . .206
Slow Cooker Carnitas 209
Game-Stopper Chili. 210
Cinnamon Blueberry French Toast. . . .213
Country Ribs Dinner 214
Applesauce Sweet Potatoes. 217
Chicken Fajita Chowder 218
Buffalo Chicken Sliders. 221
Soy-Ginger Pot Roast 222

5 INGREDIENTS

Slow Cooker Sriracha Corn

A restaurant here had been advertising Sriracha corn on the cob, but I knew I could make my own. The golden ears turned out a little sweet, a little smoky and a little hot—perfect, if you ask my three teenage boys!

—JULIE PETERSON CROFTON, MD

PREP: 15 MIN. • **COOK:** 3 HOURS
MAKES: 8 SERVINGS

½ cup butter, softened
2 tablespoons honey
1 tablespoon Sriracha Asian hot chili sauce
1 teaspoon smoked paprika
½ teaspoon kosher salt
8 small ears sweet corn, husks removed
¼ cup water
Additional smoked paprika, optional

1. Mix the first five ingredients. Place each ear of corn on a 12x12-in. piece of heavy-duty foil; spread with 1 tablespoon of the butter mixture. Wrap foil around the corn, sealing tightly. Place in a 6-qt. slow cooker.

2. Add water; cook, covered, on low until corn is tender, 3-4 hours. If desired, sprinkle the corn with additional paprika before serving.

NUTRITION FACTS 1 ear of corn: 209 cal., 13g fat (8g sat. fat), 31mg chol., 287mg sod., 24g carb. (11g sugars, 2g fiber), 4g pro.

FREEZE IT

Slow Cooker Stuffed Pepper Soup

I tweaked a recipe I got from one of my best friends, and I couldn't believe how much it really does taste like stuffed green peppers! With beef and brown rice, it makes a hearty meal on a cold day.

—GINA BAXTER PLAINFIELD, IL

PREP: 15 MIN. • **COOK:** 5 HOURS
MAKES: 12 SERVINGS (4.5 QUARTS)

- 1 pound extra-lean ground beef (95% lean)
- 1 medium onion, chopped
- 2 medium green peppers, chopped
- 1 package (8.8 ounces) ready-to-serve brown rice
- 3 tablespoons packed brown sugar
- 1/2 teaspoon salt
- 1/2 teaspoon dried basil
- 1/2 teaspoon dried oregano
- 2 cans (15 ounces each) tomato sauce
- 2 cans (14 1/2 ounces each) diced tomatoes, undrained
- 1 carton (32 ounces) beef broth

1. In a large skillet, cook and crumble beef with onion over medium heat until the meat is no longer pink, 5-7 minutes; transfer to a 6-qt. slow cooker. Stir in the remaining ingredients.

2. Cook, covered, on low until flavors are blended, 5-6 hours.

FREEZE OPTION Freeze cooled soup in freezer containers. To use, partially thaw in refrigerator overnight. Heat through in a saucepan, stirring occasionally and adding a little broth or water if necessary.

NUTRITION FACTS 1 1/2 cups: 141 cal., 3g fat (1g sat. fat), 22mg chol., 852mg sod., 18g carb. (8g sugars, 3g fiber), 11g pro.

FREEZE IT

Thai Coconut Beef

My husband and I love Thai food, but going out on weeknights can be challenging with our busy schedules. I wanted to create a Thai-inspired dinner that could double as an easy lunch the following day. Beef is fantastic in this dish, but chicken or pork would be equally delicious!

—**ASHLEY LECKER** GREEN BAY, WI

PREP: 30 MIN. • **COOK:** 7¾ HOURS
MAKES: 10 SERVINGS

- **1 boneless beef chuck roast (3 pounds), halved**
- **1 teaspoon salt**
- **1 teaspoon pepper**
- **1 large sweet red pepper, sliced**
- **1 can (13.66 ounces) coconut milk**
- **¾ cup beef stock**
- **½ cup creamy peanut butter**
- **¼ cup red curry paste**
- **2 tablespoons soy sauce**
- **2 tablespoons honey**
- **2 teaspoons minced fresh gingerroot**
- **½ pound fresh sugar snap peas, trimmed**
- **¼ cup minced fresh cilantro**
- **Hot cooked brown or white rice**
- **Optional toppings: thinly sliced green onions, chopped peanuts, hot sauce and lime wedges**

1. Sprinkle beef with salt and pepper. Place beef and pepper slices in a 5-qt. slow cooker. In a bowl, whisk coconut milk, beef stock, peanut butter, curry paste, soy sauce, honey and ginger; pour over meat. Cook, covered, on low 7-8 hours or until meat is tender.

2. Remove beef; cool slightly. Skim fat from the cooking juices. Shred beef with two forks. Return beef to slow cooker; stir in snap peas. Cook, covered, on low 45-60 minutes longer or until the peas are crisp-tender. Stir in cilantro. Serve with rice and, if desired, toppings of your choice.

FREEZE OPTION Place cooled meat mixture in freezer containers. To use, partially thaw in refrigerator overnight. Microwave, covered, on high until heated through, gently stirring and adding a little broth or water if necessary.

NUTRITION FACTS 1 cup (calculated without rice and toppings): 421 cal., 28g fat (14g sat. fat), 88mg chol., 731mg sod., 12g carb. (7g sugars, 2g fiber), 32g pro.

Slow Cooker Cheddar Bacon Ale Dip

My tangy, smoky dip won the top prize at our office party recipe contest. Other beers can work, but steer clear of dark varieties.

—**ASHLEY LECKER** GREEN BAY, WI

PREP: 15 MIN. • **COOK:** 3 HOURS
MAKES: 4½ CUPS

- 18 ounces cream cheese, softened
- ¼ cup sour cream
- 1½ tablespoons Dijon mustard
- 1 teaspoon garlic powder
- 1 cup amber beer or nonalcoholic beer
- 2 cups shredded cheddar cheese
- 1 pound bacon strips, cooked and crumbled, divided
- ¼ cup heavy whipping cream
- 1 green onion, thinly sliced
- Soft pretzel bites

1. In a greased 3-qt. slow cooker, combine cream cheese, sour cream, mustard and garlic powder until smooth. Stir in beer, cheese and all but 2 tablespoons of the bacon. Cook, covered, on low, stirring occasionally, until heated through, 3-4 hours.

2. In last 30 minutes, stir in heavy cream. Top with onion and remaining bacon. Serve with pretzel bun bites.

NUTRITION FACTS ¼ cup: 213 cal., 19g fat (10g sat. fat), 60mg chol., 378mg sod., 2g carb. (1g sugars, 0 fiber), 8g pro.

Slow Cooker Bacon Mac & Cheese

I'm all about easy slow cooker meals. Using more cheese than ever, I've developed an addictive spin on this casserole favorite.
—KRISTEN HEIGL STATEN ISLAND, NY

PREP: 20 MIN.
COOK: 3 HOURS + STANDING
MAKES: 18 SERVINGS

- **2 large eggs, lightly beaten**
- **4 cups whole milk**
- **1 can (12 ounces) evaporated milk**
- **1/4 cup butter, melted**
- **1 tablespoon all-purpose flour**
- **1 teaspoon salt**
- **1 package (16 ounces) small pasta shells**
- **1 cup shredded provolone cheese**
- **1 cup shredded Manchego or Monterey Jack cheese**
- **1 cup shredded white cheddar cheese**
- **8 bacon strips, cooked and crumbled**

1. In a large bowl, whisk the first six ingredients until blended. Stir in pasta and cheeses; transfer to a 4- or 5-qt. slow cooker.

2. Cook, covered, on low 3-3½ hours or until the pasta is tender. Turn off the slow cooker; remove insert. Let stand, uncovered, 15 minutes before serving. Top with bacon.

NUTRITION FACTS ½ cup: 272 cal., 14g fat (8g sat. fat), 59mg chol., 400mg sod., 24g carb. (5g sugars, 1g fiber), 13g pro.

Simple Swedish Meatballs

When my husband packs these saucy slow-cooked meatballs in his lunch, all his work buddies wish they had their own! They're comfort food at its easiest.

—**CHRISTINA LOGAN** GUN BARREL CITY, TX

PREP: 15 MIN. • **COOK:** 5¼ HOURS
MAKES: 10 SERVINGS

- 1 tablespoon butter
- 1 pound sliced fresh mushrooms
- 1 can (14½ ounces) reduced-sodium beef broth
- 1 can (10¾ ounces) reduced-fat reduced-sodium condensed cream of chicken soup, undiluted
- 1 envelope Lipton beefy onion soup mix
- 1 package (24 ounces) frozen fully cooked Swedish meatballs or 1 package (26 ounces) frozen fully cooked homestyle meatballs
- ⅔ cup sour cream
- 2 tablespoons minced fresh parsley or 2 teaspoons dried parsley flakes
- Hot cooked noodles or mashed potatoes, optional

1. In a large skillet, heat butter over medium-high heat; saute mushrooms until tender, 4-5 minutes. Transfer to a 4-qt. slow cooker. Stir in broth, cream of chicken soup and soup mix. Stir in meatballs. Cook, covered, on low until flavors are blended, 5-6 hours.

2. Stir in the sour cream and parsley. Cook, covered, until heated through, about 15 minutes. If desired, serve with noodles.

NUTRITION FACTS 1 cup meatballs and sauce: 295 cal., 22g fat (11g sat. fat), 46mg chol., 1045mg sod., 11g carb. (3g sugars, 3g fiber), 14g pro.

Strawberry-Banana Pudding Cake

This luscious pink pudding cake is so easy to put together. Top it with ice cream and fresh fruit, and you have one very happy family.
—NADINE MESCH MOUNT HEALTHY, OH

PREP: 15 MIN.
COOK: 3½ HOURS + STANDING
MAKES: 10 SERVINGS

- 1 package strawberry cake mix (regular size)
- 1 package (3.4 ounces) instant banana cream pudding mix
- 2 cups plain Greek yogurt
- 4 large eggs
- 1 cup water
- ¾ cup canola oil
- 2 tablespoons minced fresh basil
- 1 cup white baking chips
- Optional toppings: vanilla ice cream, sliced bananas, sliced strawberries and fresh basil

1. In a large bowl, combine the first six ingredients; beat on low speed 30 seconds. Beat on medium 2 minutes; stir in basil. Transfer to a greased 5-qt. slow cooker. Cook, covered, on low until the edges of the cake are golden brown (center will be moist), 3½-4 hours.

2. Turn off slow cooker; sprinkle cake with baking chips. Remove insert; let stand, uncovered, 10 minutes before serving. Serve warm with toppings as desired.

NUTRITION FACTS 1 serving: 373 cal., 29g fat (8g sat. fat), 90mg chol., 239mg sod., 23g carb. (21g sugars, 0 fiber), 5g pro.

FREEZE IT

Slow Cooker Carnitas

We shared these flavor-packed tacos with friends from church who came over to help us move. The slow cooker makes this recipe extra easy, and I love that whenever I make it, I'm reminded of the wonderful people back in Michigan.

—**ABIGAIL RAINES** HAMDEN, CT

PREP: 25 MIN. • **COOK:** 8 HOURS
MAKES: 12 SERVINGS

- **½ cup salsa**
- **3 bay leaves**
- **1 tablespoon salt**
- **2 teaspoons ground cumin**
- **2 teaspoons dried oregano**
- **2 teaspoons pepper**
- **1½ teaspoons garlic powder**
- **4 whole cloves**
- **1¼ cups water**
- **2 medium onions, chopped**
- **1 bone-in pork shoulder roast (6 to 7 pounds)**
- **24 corn tortillas (6 inches) or taco shells, warmed**
- **Optional toppings: shredded cheese, sour cream and chopped tomato, onion and cilantro**

1. In a small bowl, mix the first nine ingredients. Place onions in a 6-qt. oval slow cooker. Place roast over onions; pour salsa mixture over roast. Cook, covered, on low until pork is tender, 8-10 hours.

2. Remove roast; remove and discard bone. Shred pork with two forks. Serve in tortillas with toppings as desired.

FREEZE OPTION Freeze cooled pork mixture in freezer containers. To use, partially thaw in refrigerator overnight. Microwave, covered, on high in a microwave-safe dish until heated through, stirring occasionally and adding a little water or broth if necessary.

NUTRITION FACTS 2 tacos: 393 cal., 18g fat (6g sat. fat), 100mg chol., 757mg sod., 25g carb. (2g sugars, 4g fiber), 32g pro.

FREEZE IT

Game-Stopper Chili

This hearty chili with sausage, beef, beans and barley is perfect for the halftime food rush. People actually cheer when they see me coming with my slow cooker!
—**BARBARA LENTO** HOUSTON, PA

PREP: 25 MIN. • **COOK:** 6 HOURS
MAKES: 12 SERVINGS (4 QUARTS)

- 1 can (28 ounces) diced tomatoes, undrained
- 1 can (15 ounces) black beans, rinsed and drained
- 1 can (15 ounces) kidney beans, rinsed and drained
- 1 pound boneless beef chuck steak, cut into 1-inch cubes
- 1 pound bulk spicy pork sausage, cooked and drained
- 2 medium onions, chopped
- 1 medium sweet red pepper, chopped
- 1 medium green pepper, chopped
- 1 cup hot chunky salsa
- 1/3 cup medium pearl barley
- 2 tablespoons chili powder
- 2 teaspoons jarred roasted minced garlic
- 1 teaspoon salt
- 1 teaspoon ground cumin
- 4 cups beef stock
- 2 cups shredded Mexican cheese blend
- Corn chips

1. Place all ingredients except cheese and chips in a 6-qt. slow cooker. Cook, covered, on low until beef is tender, 6-8 hours.

2. Stir in cheese until melted. Serve with corn chips.

FREEZE OPTION Freeze cooled chili in freezer containers. To use, partially thaw in refrigerator overnight. Heat through in a saucepan, stirring occasionally.

NUTRITION FACTS 1 1/3 cups: 359 cal., 18g fat (7g sat. fat), 62mg chol., 1062mg sod., 26g carb. (6g sugars, 6g fiber), 23g pro

DID YOU KNOW?

Barley is the oldest domesticated grain, and has been grown for use in cooking for more than 10,000 years. It was also the basis for the first alcoholic beverages. Pearl barley is the type most commonly found in stores, and has had the hard outer hull removed.

Cinnamon Blueberry French Toast

I like to prep this breakfast in the afternoon, let it chill, then put it into the slow cooker before I go to bed. When we wake up in the morning, it's done just right.
—**ANGELA LIVELY** CONROE, TX

PREP: 15 MIN. • **COOK:** 3 HOURS
MAKES: 6 SERVINGS

- 3 large eggs
- 2 cups 2% milk
- ¼ cup sugar
- 1 teaspoon ground cinnamon
- 1 teaspoon vanilla extract
- ¼ teaspoon salt
- 9 cups cubed French bread (about 9 ounces)
- 1 cup fresh or frozen blueberries, thawed
- Maple syrup

1. Whisk together first six ingredients. Layer half of the bread in a greased 5-qt. slow cooker; top with ½ cup blueberries and half of the milk mixture. Repeat layers. Refrigerate, covered, 4 hours or overnight.

2. Cook, covered, on low until a knife inserted in the center comes out clean, 3-4 hours. Serve warm with syrup.

NOTE To increase fiber, swap whole wheat for white French bread. If you can't find whole wheat French bread, cube 100% whole wheat buns.

NUTRITION FACTS 1 cup: 265 cal., 6g fat (2g sat. fat), 100mg chol., 430mg sod., 42g carb. (18g sugars, 2g fiber), 11g pro.

Country Ribs Dinner

This is my favorite recipe for the classic ribs dinner. It's always a treat for my family when we have this.

—ROSE INGALL MANISTEE, MI

PREP: 10 MIN. • **COOK:** 6¼ HOURS
MAKES: 4 SERVINGS

- 2 pounds boneless country-style pork ribs
- ½ teaspoon salt
- ¼ teaspoon pepper
- 8 small red potatoes (about 1 pound), halved
- 4 medium carrots, cut into 1-inch pieces
- 3 celery ribs, cut into ½-inch pieces
- 1 medium onion, coarsely chopped
- ¾ cup water
- 1 garlic clove, crushed
- 1 can (10¾ ounces) condensed cream of mushroom soup, undiluted

1. Sprinkle ribs with salt and pepper; transfer to a 4-qt. slow cooker. Add potatoes, carrots, celery, onion, water and garlic. Cook, covered, on low until the meat and vegetables are tender, 6-8 hours.

2. Remove the meat and vegetables; skim fat from the cooking juices. Whisk soup into cooking juices; return the meat and vegetables to slow cooker. Cover and cook until heated through, 15-30 minutes longer.

NUTRITION FACTS 5 ounces cooked meat with 1 cup vegetables and ¼ cup gravy: 528 cal., 25g fat (8g sat. fat), 134mg chol., 1016mg sod., 30g carb. (6g sugars, 6g fiber), 43g pro.

⑤ INGREDIENTS

Applesauce Sweet Potatoes

During the holidays, using your slow cooker frees up not only oven space, but time, too! Sweet potatoes are a must on our family holiday menu, and this no-fuss version will have everyone thinking you spent hours in the kitchen.

—**PAMELA ALLEN** MARYSVILLE, OH

PREP: 15 MIN. • **COOK:** 4 HOURS
MAKES: 8 SERVINGS

- **3 pounds sweet potatoes (about 5 medium), peeled and sliced**
- **1½ cups unsweetened applesauce**
- **⅔ cup packed brown sugar**
- **3 tablespoons butter, melted**
- **1 teaspoon ground cinnamon**
- **½ cup glazed pecans, chopped, optional**

1. Place sweet potatoes in a 4-qt. slow cooker. In a small bowl, mix applesauce, brown sugar, melted butter and cinnamon; pour over potatoes.

2. Cook, covered, on low 4-5 hours or until potatoes are tender. If desired, sprinkle with pecans before serving. Serve with a slotted spoon.

NUTRITION FACTS ¾ cup (calculated without pecans): 303 cal., 5g fat (3g sat. fat), 11mg chol., 57mg sod., 65g carb. (39g sugars, 6g fiber), 3g pro.

FREEZE IT

Chicken Fajita Chowder

This south-of-the-border chowder is one of my favorite slow cooker recipes, and it's a winner at family dinners and potlucks alike. We like ours topped with fresh avocado, shredded cheddar cheese and chili cheese corn chips.

—**NANCY HEISHMAN** LAS VEGAS, NV

PREP: 20 MIN. • **COOK:** 4 HOURS
MAKES: 10 SERVINGS (3½ QUARTS)

- **3 large tomatoes, chopped**
- **1 can (15 ounces) black beans, rinsed and drained**
- **6 ounces fully cooked Spanish chorizo links, sliced**
- **2 pounds boneless skinless chicken breasts, cut into 1-inch cubes**
- **1 envelope fajita seasoning mix**
- **1½ cups frozen corn, thawed**
- **1 medium sweet red pepper, chopped**
- **1 medium green pepper, chopped**
- **6 green onions, chopped**
- **¾ cup salsa**
- **½ cup chopped fresh cilantro**
- **2 cans (14½ ounces each) reduced-sodium chicken broth**
- **1 can (10¾ ounces) condensed nacho cheese soup, undiluted**
- **Optional toppings: cubed avocado and additional cilantro**

1. Place the first 12 ingredients in a 6-qt. slow cooker. Cook, covered, on low until the chicken is tender, 4-5 hours.

2. Stir in cheese soup; heat through. If desired, top servings with avocado and additional cilantro.

FREEZE OPTION Freeze cooled soup in freezer containers. To use, partially thaw in refrigerator overnight. Heat through in a saucepan, stirring occasionally.

NUTRITION FACTS 1⅓ cups: 269 cal., 9g fat (3g sat. fat), 64mg chol., 1069mg sod., 20g carb. (5g sugars, 4g fiber), 26g pro.

FREEZE IT (5) INGREDIENTS

Buffalo Chicken Sliders

I came up with the idea for these sliders after my mom and dad made a similar recipe for a family get-together. To make it special, I sometimes use several different styles of Buffalo sauce and let guests mix and match their favorites.

—**CHRISTINA ADDISON** BLANCHESTER, OH

PREP: 20 MIN. • **COOK:** 3 HOURS
MAKES: 6 SERVINGS

- **1 pound boneless skinless chicken breasts**
- **2 tablespoons plus 1⁄3 cup Louisiana-style hot sauce, divided**
- **1⁄4 teaspoon pepper**
- **1⁄4 cup butter, cubed**
- **1⁄4 cup honey**
- **12 Hawaiian sweet rolls, warmed**
- **Optional toppings: lettuce leaves, sliced tomato, thinly sliced red onion and crumbled blue cheese**

1. Place chicken in a 3-qt. slow cooker. Toss with 2 tablespoons hot sauce and pepper; cook, covered, on low until tender, 3-4 hours.

2. Remove chicken; discard the cooking juices. In a small saucepan, combine butter, honey and remaining hot sauce; cook and stir over medium heat until blended. Shred chicken with two forks; stir into sauce and heat through. Serve on rolls with optional ingredients as desired.

FREEZE OPTION Freeze the cooled chicken mixture in freezer containers. To use, partially thaw in refrigerator overnight. Microwave, covered, on high in a microwave-safe dish until heated through, stirring occasionally; add a little water or broth if necessary.

NUTRITION FACTS 2 sliders: 396 cal., 15g fat (8g sat. fat), 92mg chol., 873mg sod., 44g carb. (24g sugars, 2g fiber), 24g pro.

Soy-Ginger Pot Roast

My husband really likes roast beef, and I really like my slow cooker. I brought in Asian influences for an all-day pot roast with some oomph.

—LISA VARNER EL PASO, TX

PREP: 25 MIN. • **COOK:** 7 HOURS
MAKES: 6 SERVINGS

- 1 boneless beef chuck roast (3 to 4 pounds)
- 1 teaspoon salt
- ½ teaspoon pepper
- 1 tablespoon canola oil
- 1½ cups water
- ½ cup reduced-sodium soy sauce
- ¼ cup honey
- 3 tablespoons cider vinegar
- 3 garlic cloves, minced
- 2 teaspoons ground ginger
- 1 teaspoon ground mustard
- 1 large onion, halved and sliced
- 2 tablespoons cornstarch
- 2 tablespoons cold water

1. Sprinkle roast with salt and pepper. In a large skillet, heat oil over medium-high heat. Brown roast on all sides. Transfer meat to a 5- or 6-qt. slow cooker. In a small bowl, mix water, soy sauce, honey, vinegar, garlic, ginger and mustard; pour over meat. Top with onion. Cook, covered, on low 7-9 hours or until the meat is tender.

2. Remove roast and onion to a platter; keep warm. Transfer cooking juices to a large saucepan; skim fat. Bring cooking juices to a boil. In a small bowl, mix cornstarch and cold water until smooth; stir into cooking juices. Return to a boil; cook and stir 1-2 minutes or until thickened. Serve with the roast.

NUTRITION FACTS 6 ounces cooked beef with ½ cup gravy: 489 cal., 24g fat (9g sat. fat), 147mg chol., 1256mg sod., 19g carb. (13g sugars, 1g fiber), 46g pro.

HOW TO

SLOW-COOK A ROAST

1. Cut roasts over 3 pounds in half to ensure even cooking.
2. Trim fat from the meat before placing it in the slow cooker to avoid greasy gravy.
3. After browning the meat in a skillet, scrape the browned bits from the bottom of the skillet and add to the slow cooker.

Shortbread Lemon Tart, p. 246

CHAPTER 8

EASILY IMPRESSIVE DESSERTS

Cakes, cheesecakes, pies and more—serve up a sweet treat to finish your meal!

Raspberry Chocolate Puffs 226
Easy Berry Cheesecake Parfaits 229
Caramel Apple Cupcakes 230
Apple Dumpling Bake 233
Turtle Praline Tart 234
Rustic Pear Tart 237
Favorite Dutch Apple Pie 238
Easy Four-Layer Chocolate Dessert . . . 241
Brownie Swirl Cheesecake 242
Hot Chocolate Pumpkin Cake. 245
Shortbread Lemon Tart. 246
Blueberry Lemon Trifle 249
Coconut Macaroon Pie 250
Sacher Torte Squares 253

Raspberry Chocolate Puffs

This chocolaty, flaky dessert is one of my favorite show-off recipes because it makes a spectacular presentation. Although it looks complicated, it's actually really easy and quick to make!
—**ANNELIESE DEISING** PLYMOUTH, MI

PREP: 25 MIN. • **BAKE:** 20 MIN. + COOLING
MAKES: 8 SERVINGS

- **1 cup milk chocolate chips**
- **1 cup white baking chips**
- **1 cup chopped pecans**
- **1 package (17.3 ounces) frozen puff pastry, thawed**
- **1 package (12 ounces) frozen unsweetened raspberries, thawed**
- **1 cup confectioners' sugar**
- **Additional confectioners' sugar**
- **Optional ingredients: fresh raspberries and additional chocolate and white baking chips**

1. Preheat oven to 425°. Toss together chocolate chips, baking chips and pecans. On a lightly floured surface, roll each pastry sheet into a 12-in. square; cut each sheet into quarters, making four 6-in. squares.

2. Place squares on ungreased baking sheets; top each with about ⅓ cup chocolate mixture. Lightly brush edges of pastry with water; bring together all corners, pinching seams to seal.

3. Bake the mixture until golden brown, 18-20 minutes. Remove to a wire rack to cool slightly. Puree frozen raspberries with 1 cup confectioners' sugar in a food processor. Strain to remove seeds.

4. To serve, dust pastries with confectioners' sugar. Serve with raspberry sauce and, if desired, fresh berries and additional chips.

NUTRITION FACTS 1 serving: 699 cal., 39g fat (13g sat. fat), 9mg chol., 238mg sod., 81g carb. (40g sugars, 7g fiber), 9g pro.

Easy Berry Cheesecake Parfaits

These sweet little parfaits take everything that's good about cheesecake and make it way easier. You get the rich creaminess, graham cracker crunch and bright berry flavor all in a fun individual portion.

—*TASTE OF HOME* TEST KITCHEN

START TO FINISH: 15 MIN.
MAKES: 2 SERVINGS

- **2 ounces cream cheese, softened**
- **⅔ cup marshmallow creme**
- **½ cup frozen whipped topping**
- **4 tablespoons graham cracker crumbs**
- **1 cup fresh raspberries**
- **1 cup fresh blueberries**

1. Beat cream cheese and marshmallow creme until blended; fold in whipped topping.

2. Sprinkle 2 tablespoons cracker crumbs into each of two glasses or dessert dishes. Layer each with ½ cup cream cheese mixture, ¼ cup raspberries and ¼ cup blueberries; repeat the layers. Refrigerate, covered, until ready to serve.

NUTRITION FACTS 1 parfait: 396 cal., 15g fat (9g sat. fat), 29mg chol., 174mg sod., 54g carb. (39g sugars, 6g fiber), 4g pro.

Caramel Apple Cupcakes

Bring these extra-special cupcakes to your next event and watch how quickly they disappear! With a caramel topping and spice-cake base, they're the perfect mix of two fall-favorite treats.

—DIANE HALFERTY CORPUS CHRISTI, TX

PREP: 25 MIN. • **BAKE:** 20 MIN. + COOLING
MAKES: 1 DOZEN

- **1 package spice or carrot cake mix (regular size)**
- **2 cups chopped peeled tart apples (about 2 medium)**
- **20 caramels**
- **3 tablespoons 2% milk**
- **1 cup finely chopped pecans, toasted**
- **12 wooden skewers (4½ inch)**

1. Preheat oven to 350°. Line 12 jumbo muffin cups with paper liners.

2. Prepare the cake mix batter according to package directions; fold in apples. Fill prepared cups three-fourths full. Bake until a toothpick inserted in center comes out clean, about 20 minutes. Cool 10 minutes before removing from pans; cool completely on a wire rack.

3. In a small saucepan, cook caramels and milk over low heat until smooth, stirring constantly. Spread over the cupcakes. Sprinkle with pecans. Insert a wooden skewer in each.

NOTE To toast nuts, bake in a shallow pan in a 350° oven for 5-10 minutes or cook in a skillet over low heat until lightly browned, stirring occasionally.

NUTRITION FACTS 1 cupcake: 365 cal., 19g fat (3g sat. fat), 48mg chol., 315mg sod., 48g carb. (30g sugars, 1g fiber), 5g pro.

Apple Dumpling Bake

I received this recipe from a friend of mine, then tweaked it to suit my family's tastes. Mountain Dew is the secret ingredient in this rich apple dessert that's a snap to make.

—**CHRIS SHIELDS** MONROVIA, IN

PREP: 15 MIN. • **BAKE:** 35 MIN.
MAKES: 8 SERVINGS

- 2 medium Granny Smith apples
- 2 tubes (8 ounces each) refrigerated crescent rolls
- 1 cup sugar
- ⅓ cup butter, softened
- ½ teaspoon ground cinnamon
- ¾ cup Mountain Dew soda
- Vanilla ice cream

1. Preheat oven to 350°. Peel, core and cut each apple into eight wedges. Unroll both tubes of crescent dough; separate each into eight triangles. Wrap a triangle around each wedge. Place in a greased 13x9-in. baking dish.

2. In a bowl, mix sugar, butter and cinnamon until blended; sprinkle over dumplings. Slowly pour soda around the rolls (do not stir).

3. Bake, uncovered, until golden brown and apples are tender, 35-40 minutes. Serve warm with ice cream.

NUTRITION FACTS 2 dumplings: 414 cal., 20g fat (9g sat. fat), 20mg chol., 510mg sod., 55g carb. (35g sugars, 1g fiber), 4g pro.

(5) INGREDIENTS

Turtle Praline Tart

This rich dessert is my own creation, and I'm very proud of it. It's easy enough to make for every day but special enough to serve guests or take to a potluck.

—**KATHY SPECHT** CLINTON, MT

PREP: 35 MIN. + CHILLING
MAKES: 16 SERVINGS

- **1 sheet refrigerated pie pastry**
- **36 caramels**
- **1 cup heavy whipping cream, divided**
- **3½ cups pecan halves**
- **½ cup semisweet chocolate chips, melted**

1. Preheat oven to 450°. Unroll pastry on a lightly floured surface. Transfer to an 11-in. fluted tart pan with removable bottom; trim the edges.

2. Line unpricked pastry shell with a double thickness of heavy-duty foil. Bake for 8 minutes. Remove foil; bake for 5-6 minutes longer or until light golden brown. Cool on a wire rack.

3. In a large saucepan, combine caramels and ½ cup cream. Cook and stir over medium-low heat until caramels are melted. Stir in pecans. Spread the filling evenly into the crust. Drizzle with melted chocolate.

4. Refrigerate 30 minutes or until set. Whip remaining cream; serve with tart.

NUTRITION FACTS 1 slice: 335 cal., 24g fat (4g sat. fat), 4mg chol., 106mg sod., 31g carb. (19g sugars, 3g fiber), 4g pro.

Rustic Pear Tart

I saw a recipe for this rustic tart and wanted to try my own version of it. I changed the spices and chose my own fruits. It is a great dessert for the fall.

—LISA VARNER EL PASO, TX

PREP: 20 MIN. • **BAKE:** 35 MIN. + COOLING
MAKES: 8 SERVINGS

- 1 sheet refrigerated pie pastry
- 4 cups thinly sliced peeled fresh pears
- 1/4 cup dried cherries
- 1 teaspoon vanilla extract
- 4 tablespoons sugar, divided
- 4 teaspoons cornstarch
- 1 teaspoon ground cinnamon
- 1/2 teaspoon ground ginger
- 1/4 cup chopped walnuts
- 1 large egg white
- 1 tablespoon water

1. Preheat oven to 375°. On a lightly floured surface, roll out pastry into a 14-in. circle. Transfer to a parchment paper-lined baking sheet; set aside.

2. In a large bowl, combine the pears, the cherries and vanilla extract. Combine 3 tablespoons sugar, cornstarch, cinnamon and ginger; sprinkle over pear mixture and stir gently to combine. Spoon over pastry to within 2 in. of edges; sprinkle with walnuts. Fold edges of pastry over filling, leaving center uncovered.

3. Beat egg white and water; brush over folded pastry. Sprinkle with remaining sugar. Bake for 35-40 minutes or until crust is golden and filling is bubbly. Using parchment paper, slide tart onto a wire rack to cool.

NUTRITION FACTS 1 piece: 239 cal., 10g fat (3g sat. fat), 5mg chol., 107mg sod., 37g carb. (18g sugars, 2g fiber), 3g pro.

Favorite Dutch Apple Pie

Everything about this dessert makes it the top request for family gatherings. Its oat crust reminds me of a cookie, and the tart apple filling just can't be beat during harvest time.

—**BRENDA DUFRESNE** MIDLAND, MI

PREP: 20 MIN. • **BAKE:** 40 MIN. + COOLING
MAKES: 8 SERVINGS

- 2 cups all-purpose flour
- 1 cup packed brown sugar
- ½ cup quick-cooking oats
- ¾ cup butter, melted

FILLING

- ⅔ cup sugar
- 3 tablespoons cornstarch
- 1¼ cups cold water
- 4 cups chopped peeled tart apples (about 2 large)
- 1 teaspoon vanilla extract

1. Preheat oven to 350°. Mix flour, brown sugar, oats and butter; reserve 1½ cups mixture for topping. Press remaining mixture onto bottom and up sides of an ungreased 9-in. pie plate.

2. In a large saucepan, mix the sugar, cornstarch and water until smooth; bring to a boil. Cook and stir until thickened, about 2 minutes. Remove from heat; stir in apples and vanilla. Pour into crust. Crumble topping over filling.

3. Bake until crust is golden brown and filling is bubbly, 40-45 minutes. Cool on a wire rack.

NUTRITION FACTS 1 piece: 494 cal., 18g fat (11g sat. fat), 46mg chol., 146mg sod., 81g carb. (49g sugars, 2g fiber), 4g pro.

Easy Four-Layer Chocolate Dessert

I grew up on these nutty, chocolaty layered treats. Now I make them for both my mom and myself, because she loves them, too.
—KRISTEN STECKLEIN WAUKESHA, WI

PREP: 25 MIN. • **BAKE:** 15 MIN. + COOLING
MAKES: 15 SERVINGS

- 1 cup all-purpose flour
- ½ cup cold butter
- 1 cup chopped walnuts, toasted, divided
- 1 package (8 ounces) cream cheese, softened
- 1 cup confectioners' sugar
- 2 cartons (8 ounces each) frozen whipped topping, thawed, divided
- 2½ cups 2% milk
- 2 packages (3.9 ounces each) instant chocolate pudding mix
- 1 cup semisweet chocolate chunks
- Chocolate syrup

1. Preheat oven to 350°. Place flour in a small bowl; cut in butter until crumbly. Stir in ½ cup walnuts. Press onto bottom of an ungreased 13x9-in. baking dish. Bake until light golden brown, 12-15 minutes. Cool completely on a wire rack.

2. In a small bowl, beat cream cheese and confectioners' sugar until smooth; fold in one carton of whipped topping. Spread over the crust. In a large bowl, whisk milk and pudding mix 2 minutes. Gently spread over the cream cheese layer. Top with remaining whipped topping. Sprinkle with chocolate chunks and the remaining walnuts. Refrigerate until cold.

3. Cut into bars. Just before serving, drizzle with chocolate syrup.

NOTE To toast nuts, bake in a shallow pan in a 350° oven for 5-10 minutes or cook in a skillet over low heat until lightly browned, stirring occasionally.

NUTRITION FACTS 1 piece: 434 cal., 26g fat (15g sat. fat), 36mg chol., 195mg sod., 46g carb. (27g sugars, 2g fiber), 5g pro.

Brownie Swirl Cheesecake

It may look fancy, but this cheesecake is so simple. The secret is the speedy crust—it's from a packaged brownie mix! You don't need to be an experienced cook to make the elegant chocolate swirls on top; anyone can do it.

—**JANET BRUNNER** BURLINGTON, KY

PREP: 10 MIN. • **BAKE:** 50 MIN. + CHILLING
MAKES: 8-10 SERVINGS

- **1 package (8 ounces) brownie mix**
- **2 packages (8 ounces each) cream cheese, softened**
- **½ cup sugar**
- **1 teaspoon vanilla extract**
- **2 large eggs**
- **1 cup milk chocolate chips, melted**
- **Whipped cream and miniature chocolate kisses, optional**

1. Prepare brownie mix according to package directions for chewy fudge brownies. Spread into a greased 9-in. springform pan. Bake at 350° for 15 minutes (brownies will not test done). Cool for 10 minutes on a wire rack.

2. Meanwhile, in a bowl, combine the cream cheese, sugar and vanilla. Add eggs, one at a time, beating well after each addition.

3. Pour over the brownie crust. Top with melted chocolate; cut through batter with a knife to swirl the chocolate.

4. Bake at 350° for 35-40 minutes or until center is almost set. Run a knife around edge of pan to loosen; cool completely. Remove sides of pan; refrigerate for at least 3 hours. Garnish with whipped cream and chocolate kisses if desired.

PER SERVING 1 each: 314 cal., 17g fat (9g sat. fat), 72mg chol., 182mg sodium, 38g carb. (30g sugars, 1g fiber), 5g pro.

Hot Chocolate Pumpkin Cake

Hot chocolate is my go-to indulgence in winter. To go with it, I like this moist pumpkin cake dusted with cocoa for an extra chocolate boost.

—**COLLEEN DELAWDER** HERNDON, VA

PREP: 20 MIN.
BAKE: 55 MINUTES + COOLING
MAKES: 16 SERVINGS

- 1 can (15 ounces) pumpkin
- 2 cups sugar
- 3 large eggs
- ½ cup packed brown sugar
- ½ cup butter, melted
- ½ cup canola oil
- 1 tablespoon vanilla extract
- 3 cups all-purpose flour
- 2 teaspoons baking soda
- 2 teaspoons ground cinnamon
- ¼ teaspoon ground nutmeg
- ¼ teaspoon ground chipotle pepper
- ½ teaspoon salt
- 1 package (12 ounces) miniature semisweet chocolate chips
- Baking cocoa or confectioners' sugar, optional

1. Preheat oven to 350°. Generously grease and flour a 10-in. fluted tube pan.

2. Beat first seven ingredients until well blended. In another bowl, whisk together flour, baking soda, spices and salt; gradually beat into the pumpkin mixture. Stir in chocolate chips.

3. Add batter to prepared pan. Bake until a toothpick inserted in the center comes out clean, 55-65 minutes. Cool in pan 30 minutes before removing to a wire rack to cool completely. If desired, dust with cocoa.

NUTRITION FACTS 1 slice: 450 cal., 20g fat (8g sat. fat), 50mg chol., 298mg sod., 66g carb. (45g sugars, 3g fiber), 5g pro.

Shortbread Lemon Tart

For a change from ordinary lemon bars, we added orange zest to both the crust and filling and turned the recipe into a tart.
—***TASTE OF HOME* TEST KITCHEN**

PREP: 20 MIN. • **BAKE:** 25 MIN. + COOLING
MAKES: 10 SERVINGS

- 3 large eggs
- 1¼ cups granulated sugar
- ¼ cup lemon juice
- 1 tablespoon grated orange zest
- ¼ cup butter, melted

CRUST

- 1 cup all-purpose flour
- ⅓ cup confectioners' sugar
- ½ cup ground almonds
- 1 teaspoon grated lemon zest
- 1 teaspoon grated orange zest
- ½ cup cold butter, cubed
- Additional confectioners' sugar
- Fresh raspberries, optional

1. Let eggs stand at room temperature for 30 minutes.

2. Preheat oven to 350°. Whisk together eggs, sugar, lemon juice and orange zest. Whisk in butter until smooth. Set aside.

3. For crust, pulse first six ingredients in a food processor until mixture forms a ball. Press pastry onto the bottom and up the sides of an ungreased 9-in. fluted tart pan with removable bottom.

4. Pour lemon mixture into crust. Bake until center is almost set, 25-30 minutes. Cool on a wire rack. Just before serving, sprinkle with confectioners' sugar and, if desired, fresh raspberries.

NUTRITION FACTS 1 slice: 330 cal., 18g fat (9g sat. fat), 101mg chol., 158mg sod., 40g carb. (29g sugars, 1g fiber), 4g pro.

5 INGREDIENTS

Blueberry Lemon Trifle

A refreshing lemon filling and fresh blueberries give this sunny dessert sensation plenty of color. Don't worry about heating up the oven—this trifle doesn't require baking.
—**ELLEN PEDEN** HOUSTON, TX

PREP: 15 MIN. + CHILLING
MAKES: 12-14 SERVINGS

- **3 cups fresh blueberries, divided**
- **2 cans (15¾ ounces each) lemon pie filling**
- **2 cups (8 ounces) lemon yogurt**
- **1 prepared angel food cake (8 to 10 ounces), cut into 1-inch cubes**
- **1 carton (8 ounces) frozen whipped topping, thawed**
- **Lemon slices and fresh mint, optional**

1. Set aside ¼ cup blueberries for garnish. In a large bowl, combine pie filling and yogurt.

2. In a 3½-qt. serving or trifle bowl, layer a third of the cake cubes, lemon mixture and blueberries. Repeat layers twice. Top with whipped topping. Cover and refrigerate for at least 2 hours. Garnish with reserved blueberries, and lemon and mint if desired.

NUTRITION FACTS 273 cal., 5g fat (3g sat. fat), 43mg chol., 277mg sod., 52g carb. (43g sugars, 1g fiber), 4g pro.

Coconut Macaroon Pie

Coconut macaroons are divine, but they can be a little messy to make. I turned the batter into a pie filling, and the luscious results speak for themselves.

—BECKY MOLLENKAMP ST. LOUIS, MO

PREP: 15 MIN. • **BAKE:** 35 MIN.
MAKES: 10 SERVINGS

- 1 sheet refrigerated pie pastry
- 2 large eggs
- 1 can (14 ounces) sweetened condensed milk
- 1/4 cup butter, melted
- 1 teaspoon almond extract
- 1/4 teaspoon salt
- 1/4 cup all-purpose flour
- 1 package (14 ounces) sweetened shredded coconut

1. Preheat oven to 350°. Unroll pastry sheet into a 9-in. pie plate; flute edge. Refrigerate while preparing filling.

2. In a large bowl, beat eggs, milk, melted butter, extract and salt until blended. Stir in flour. Reserve 1/2 cup coconut; stir the remaining coconut into the egg mixture. Transfer to pastry-lined pie plate. Sprinkle with reserved coconut.

3. Bake on a lower oven rack for 35-45 minutes or until golden brown and filling is set. Cool on a wire rack.

NUTRITION FACTS 1 piece: 490 cal., 29g fat (20g sat. fat), 67mg chol., 344mg sod., 53g carb. (40g sugars, 2g fiber), 7g pro.

Sacher Torte Squares

Sacher torte is a Viennese cake that requires several steps. My squares are an easy alternative, but they still feature the classic apricot and chocolate flavors.
—**ARLENE ERLBACH** MORTON GROVE, IL

PREP: 30 MIN. • **BAKE:** 30 MIN. + CHILLING
MAKES: 20 SERVINGS

- 1 package devil's food cake mix (regular size)
- 2 cans (12 ounces each) apricot cake and pastry filling
- 3 large eggs
- 2 teaspoons vanilla extract
- 1 cup (6 ounces) dark chocolate chips

TOPPINGS

- ½ cup apricot preserves
- 2 teaspoons vanilla extract
- ⅓ cup butter, cubed
- 1 cup sugar
- 1 cup heavy whipping cream
- 1 cup (6 ounces) dark chocolate chips
- ¼ cup sliced almonds

1. Preheat oven to 350°. Grease a 13x9-in. baking pan.

2. In a large bowl, combine cake mix, apricot filling, eggs and vanilla; beat on low speed 30 seconds. Beat on medium for 2 minutes. Fold in chocolate chips. Transfer to prepared pan. Bake for 30-35 minutes or until a toothpick inserted in the center comes out clean.

3. Remove pan from oven and place on a wire rack. In a small bowl, mix preserves and vanilla; spread over warm cake.

4. In a small saucepan, combine butter, sugar and cream; bring to a boil, stirring to dissolve sugar. Remove from heat; stir in chocolate chips until melted. Spread over cake; sprinkle with almonds. Refrigerate until set, about 1 hour.

NUTRITION FACTS 1 piece: 410 cal., 17g fat (10g sat. fat), 52mg chol., 275mg sod., 64g carb. (45g sugars, 3g fiber), 4g pro.

RECIPE INDEX

A

Almond Strawberry Salad, 148
Apple Dumpling Bake, 233
Apple-Glazed Chicken Thighs, 94
Applesauce Sweet Potatoes, 217
Artichoke Blue Cheese Fettuccine, 81
Asian Chicken Rice Bowl, 108
Asparagus Beef Lo Mein, 111

B

Bacon & Cheddar Chicken, 89
Bacon Avocado Salad, 155
Bacon-Wrapped Pesto Pork Tenderloin, 86
Berries in Yogurt Cream, 32
Black Bean Turkey Chili, 40
Blue Cheese Chicken Salad Sandwiches, 164
Blue Cheese Potato Chips, 27
Blueberry Lemon Trifle, 249
Broccoli Slaw, 35
Brownie Swirl Cheesecake, 242
Bucatini with Sausage & Kale, 74
Buffalo Chicken Sliders, 221

C

Cannellini Bean Hummus, 8
Caprese Salad Kabobs, 36
Caramel Apple Cupcakes, 230
Cashew Turkey Salad Sandwiches, 180
Cheesy Broccoli Soup in a Bread Bowl, 168
Cheesy Cheddar Broccoli Casserole, 147
Chicken Enchilada Bake, 124
Chicken Fajita Chowder, 218
Cilantro Lime Shrimp, 67
Cinnamon Blueberry French Toast, 213
Cobb Salad Sub, 24
Coconut Macaroon Pie, 250
Colcannon Irish Potatoes, 132
Cold-Day Chicken Noodle Soup, 179
Country Ribs Dinner, 214
Creamy Lemon Rice, 151
Cucumbers with Dressing, 23
Curried Chicken Corn Chowder, 187
Curried Egg Salad, 175

E

Easy Berry Cheesecake Parfaits, 229
Easy Four-Layer Chocolate Dessert, 241

F

Fabulous Green Beans, 144
Favorite Dutch Apple Pie, 238

G

Game-Stopper Chili, 210
Garlic Shrimp & Rice Salad, 127
Glazed Smoked Chops with Pears, 43
Greek Couscous Salad, 60
Grilled Basil Chicken and Tomatoes, 93
Grilled Chicken, Mango & Blue Cheese Tortillas, 47
Grilled Eggplant Sandwiches, 52
Grilled Flank Steak, 78
Grilled Garden Pizza, 64
Grilled Peach, Rice & Arugula Salad, 143
Grilled Tilapia Piccata, 77

H

Hot Chocolate Pumpkin Cake, 245

I

Indian Spiced Chickpea Wraps, 167
Italian Joes on Texas Toast, 63
Italian Wedding Soup, 176

J

Jalapeno Burgers with Gorgonzola, 171
Jalapeno Popper Mexican Street Corn, 44

L

Lemon Garlic Mushrooms, 159
Lemony Chicken & Rice, 115
Lemony Chicken Soup, 183
Lemon-Parsley Tilapia, 85

M

Maple-Dijon Chicken, 56
Mushroom & Onion Grilled Cheese Sandwiches, 188
Mushroom Bacon Turkey Burgers, 184

N

Nuts & Seeds Trail Mix, 19

O

Olive & Onion Quick Bread, 156
One-Pan Tuscan Ravioli , 112

P

Parmesan Roasted Broccoli, 135
Penne & Smoked Sausage, 103
Pierogi Chicken Supper, 70
Pina Colada Dip, 12
Pizza in a Bowl, 59
Pork Chops with Honey-Garlic Sauce, 73

Q

Quick Cream of Mushroom Soup, 191

R

Raspberry Chocolate Puffs, 226
Roasted Red Pepper Tapenade, 16

Roasted Vegetables with Sage, 140
Rosemary Shrimp with Spaghetti, 104
Rustic Pear Tart, 237

S

Sacher Torte Squares, 253
Sausage-Stuffed Butternut Squash, 100
Savory Beer Pork Chops, 90
Shortbread Lemon Tart, 246
Shrimp Gazpacho, 172
Simple Swedish Meatballs, 205
Skillet Ham & Rice, 120
Slow Cooker Bacon Mac & Cheese, 202
Slow Cooker Carnitas, 209
Slow Cooker Cheddar Bacon Ale Dip, 201
Slow Cooker Sriracha Corn, 194
Slow Cooker Stuffed Pepper Soup, 197
Snappy Tuna Melts, 11
Southwest-Style Wedding Soup, 51
Soy-Ginger Pot Roast, 222
Spaghetti Squash Meatball Casserole, 107
Spicy Cajun Sausage & Rice Skillet, 123
Spicy Peanut Chicken & Noodles, 119
Spinach Blueberry Salad, 15
Spring Asparagus, 152
Strawberry-Banana Pudding Cake, 206
Strawberry Watermelon Slush, 28
Sun-Dried Tomato Garlic Bread, 31

T

Taco Noodle Dish, 116
Tandoori Chicken Pita Pizzas, 128
Tarragon Asparagus Salad, 139
Thai Coconut Beef, 198
Three-Bean Baked Beans, 136
Tortellini Carbonara, 97
Turtle Praline Tart, 234

V

Vegetarian Pad Thai, 55

W

White Cheddar Mac & Cheese, 48

Y

Yummy Corn Chip Salad, 160

Z

Zesty Grilled Ham, 82